In my early days as a leader, if I had known myself better, I would have made better decisions. Self-knowledge is priceless, and in this book Clay helps you move beyond the distractions to a moment-to-moment awareness that can help you regulate the way you think, act, and feel.

IAN MORGAN CRON, author of the popular
Enneagram book *The Road Back to You*

Let's be honest . . . we live in a world *filled* with distractions. And you don't even have to go looking for them. They'll find you! But experiencing genuine momentum means stopping distractions in their tracks. And that's what makes *How to Lead in a World of Distraction* such a valuable resource—not just for leaders but for anyone longing to make a difference in the world.

DAVE RAMSEY, bestselling author and
nationally syndicated radio show host

This book provides practical ways to help you focus on what's most important and to grow as a leader.

COLIN FAULKNER, SVP, sales and
marketing, Chicago Cubs

The first time I heard Clay speak on this topic, I thought, *This should be a book*. And now it is. Noise is inevitable. Noise is distracting. In this book Clay provides leaders with practical ways to turn down the noise personally and organizationally.

ANDY STANLEY, senior pastor and
founder, North Point Ministries

HOW TO LEAD IN A WORLD OF DISTRACTION

HOW TO LEAD IN A WORLD OF DISTRACTION

MAXIMIZING YOUR INFLUENCE BY TURNING DOWN THE NOISE

CLAY SCROGGINS

ZONDERVAN REFLECTIVE

ZONDERVAN REFLECTIVE

How to Lead in a World of Distraction
Copyright © 2019 by Clay Scroggins

ISBN 978-0-310-59869-5 (hardcover)

ISBN 978-0-310-59874-9 (international trade paper edition)

ISBN 978-0-310-59873-2 (audio)

ISBN 978-0-310-59870-1 (ebook)

Requests for information should be addressed to:
Zondervan, 3900 *Sparks Dr. SE, Grand Rapids, Michigan 49546*

Cover design: Thinkpen Design
Interior design: Denise Froehlich

Printed in the United States of America

19 20 21 22 23 /LSC/ 10 9 8 7 6 5 4 3 2 1

Jenny, your being who you are makes
me want to be a better me

CONTENTS

ACKNOWLEDGMENTS

Anything worth something in life is always some sort of group effort. This book is no different. So I'd like to kick some shout-outs to a few people who have made this project possible.

For my wife and kids:

Jenny, you really are my ride-or-die. You are such an encourager for me, but you're also not afraid to give me the slap-in-the-butt I need for just a little more hustle. Thanks for graciously pushing me, patiently waiting for me, and always believing in me.

Lucy, Jake, Sally, Cooper, and Whit: out of the whole lineup, I'd choose each of you every time.

For those at work who've helped me so much:

Megan Gross, I still can't believe you took the job twelve years ago, but I'm so glad you did. You keep it all straight, you treat everyone so well, and you make it all so fun. Thank you!

Suzy Gray, you're almost always the smartest, hardest working, and most strategic person in the room, but you act like you don't even know it. I owe you and Brooklyn so much because of all you've done for me. Thank you!

Andy Stanley, thanks for giving me a chance all those years ago. Thanks for being the most respectable pastor on the planet. Anyone else with your amount of power and fame has become pretty weird, but you just seem to stay on your knees.

Lane Jones, thanks for teaching me that it is possible to be friends with your boss. You're a terrific leader and a great boss!

Justin Elam, thanks for helping me shape these thoughts at the very beginning.

Evan McLaughlin, thanks for always letting me run stuff by you at the very last minute.

Mallory and Adam Boyle, you two were there for the beginning of this, and I'm so grateful for you both!

Jonny Wills, thanks for being so easy to work with and for doing such great work. You're a good man but also a talented man. I'm super grateful for you!

Debbie Causey, you've taught me so much about emotional health because you are just so emotionally healthy. Thank you!

The publishing team at Zondervan has been so amazing to work with.

Ryan Pazdur, you're a phenomenal editor, but you're way more than that. You're smart, hardworking, intuitive, and creative. More than anything, though, you took this project so personally. You were in it with me, and I can't thank you enough!

Nate Kroeze, books aren't that helpful if they don't get into people's hands, and you're so good at that part. Keep carving out your own lane. You're one of a kind.

Kim Tanner and Dawn Hurley, you're like the Mariano Rivera of this process. You both came in at the end and made it all so much better.

Jesse Hillman, thanks for handling the tough stuff with grace and wisdom.

Oh, and Stan Gundry, you're a legend. I'm still waiting on a ride in that precious car of yours.

CHAPTER 1

THE DANGER OF THE DISTRACTION

I'm so easily distracted.

Last year, my ever-adventurous in-laws from Texas were coming to Atlanta for a visit. Instead of hitting up the same attractions they had done every year with our kids, they asked us if we would want to explore a new city, one within easy driving distance of our home. My wife and her mom got together and planned a short trip to Chattanooga, a pretty cool city with great downtown activities for kids.

It was a hot summer evening in July, and after a busy day at work, I pulled my recently purchased Ford Explorer into the driveway of the rental house we'd booked a few blocks north of Chattanooga. I was the first to arrive, and the owner of the home (who lived right next door) was already there, waiting in the driveway to greet me. Even though the sun hadn't set, the sky was growing dark. A significant thunderstorm was brewing. As soon as I opened my car door to say hello, huge drops of rain began falling. I raced to the front door of the house and followed the owner inside for a quick tour.

Ten minutes later, my wife, our kids, and my in-laws arrived. Our five young kids raced into the house like it was the grand opening of a Chuck E. Cheese and they were giving away free tickets to the first customers. They were excited, to say the least. I kissed my wife, greeted her parents (whom I hadn't seen in a few months), and introduced everyone to Jim, the homeowner. The scene was a little chaotic with everyone suddenly filling the empty house, kids racing around, and multiple conversations taking place. It reminded me of the opening scene of *Home Alone*.

After the greetings and salutations, I made a handoff to my wife so she could download the remaining details about the house from the owner. I hate details. My eyes were already glazing over as Jim dove deeper into the finer points of the ridiculously complicated home theater system. I pointed to the three-ring binder he was showing me. It had all the instructions for anything we would ever want to use. It didn't mean anything to me at the time, but I vaguely remember when the circus arrived and he was in the middle of telling me about a gate at the front of the driveway. It was in working order, but it hadn't been used in a while. But I was hardly listening at this point. There were simply too many distractions.

"You're welcome to use the gate if you want, but I don't see any reason to," he foreshadowed. I nodded my head in affirmation, but my mind was distracted by his odd resemblance to an odd combination of Bill Wennington, the former Chicago Bulls player, and Walter White from *Breaking Bad*.

As I said, I'm easily distracted.

Even though it was only 7:00 p.m., our youngest child, Whit, who was six months old at the time, was letting us know he was ready for bed. So before I unpacked the rest of my wife's van, I wrestled with the pack-n-play, cramming it into the closet like an all-pro dad. I de-escalated a confrontation between two of our older kids and confiscated the dart set they had found in the basement. That seemed safe. After finishing the rest of the unloading process, I assisted my wife with bath time for the little ones, helped our older kids locate a place to sleep, convinced the one still bleeding from the badly thrown dart that a band-aid was not needed because it was merely a flesh wound, and then collapsed into bed around 10:00 p.m. After all, I had to get up at 5:00 a.m. to make the two-hour drive back to work because I had a meeting the next morning I just couldn't miss.

Or so I thought.

As I do every morning, I woke up without my alarm and jumped right in the shower. I remember having a random thought as I was looking through my overnight bag for a toothbrush.

Where did I put my car keys?

I retraced the previous night in my head—the storm, the homeowner conversations, the in-law greetings, and the juggling act to get the kids settled. I couldn't remember doing anything with them. I must have left them in the car.

Hmmm. That probably wasn't smart.

Stepping outside into that dark, muggy Chattanooga morning was a moment I'll never forget.

Weird. Where's my car?

Didn't I park in the driveway? I was sure I did.

Would my wife or my in-laws have moved it? I could think of no reason for them to have done that. Could my kids have moved it? If they had, I wouldn't even be mad. That would be impressive.

And then it hit me. I *had* left my keys in the car. I had been so distracted by the flurry of arriving and unloading that I left them in the ignition. And now my car had been stolen.

Distractions are a problem.

EVERYONE, EVERYWHERE

None of us are immune to the growing cacophony of distractions all around us. Over the last few years, I've asked many people a simple question: Are there more or fewer distractions in our world today than there were ten years ago? The answer is always a resounding, "More!" We all feel it. And we are drowning in them everywhere we go.

It's a problem in the workplace as employers face a distraction epidemic. In 2016 CareerBuilder conducted a survey on the topic of distractions, asking two thousand hiring and HR managers to identify the top culprits of workplace distractions. The most common answers aren't surprising: smartphones (55 percent), the internet (41 percent), gossip (37 percent), social media (37 percent), coworkers dropping by (27 percent), smoking or snack breaks (27 percent), email (26 percent), meetings (24 percent), and noisy coworkers (20 percent).[1] Even worse is the direct effect these distractions have on productivity: "Three in four employers (75 percent) say two or more hours a day are lost in productivity because employees are distracted. Forty-three percent say at least three hours a day are lost." Look again at that list. Several of the items mentioned as common distractions are *recent* problems, the result of shifting technology, and most employers are still trying to determine their cost. But one thing is clear. There is a cost. And the distractions we face in the workplace are only getting worse.

Work isn't the only place we face distractions, though. It's an epidemic in our homes as well. I have too many stories of missing something in my kids' lives because my mind was consumed with something else. I'm distracted and not always present, even when I'm in the same room as my family. I might be mulling over a problem at work, or I could be distracted by my Twitter feed. Put this in the category of "Parenting Fails." Just last week, my wife and I were managing bath time for our little kids when we lost one of them. It was only for five minutes, so please hold your judgment until you hear the full story.

Our youngest son, Whit, is still learning to walk, and he was finished with his bath and ready for bed. By ready for bed, I mean he was waiting on me to put on his diaper and pajamas. Evidently, he had waited long enough. I was distracted, fixing something on the camera in his room, and somehow I didn't notice him quietly crawling away. In the middle of helping another kid with some surprisingly difficult homework, my wife yelled at me from the other room, "Will you put Whit to bed?" To her credit, my wife is a stickler for bedtime, and since it was a few minutes past 7:00 p.m., she was keenly aware he was already late.

I looked around to find him and then realized he was gone. No problem. I was sure he had found a tube of toothpaste and was creatively decorating the bathroom walls with it (insert eye roll emoji). Since the gate on the stairs was wide open, I headed downstairs. I looked in every room, but I couldn't find him anywhere.

That's when I noticed that the door leading outside was wide open. That was odd. Surely he hadn't gone outside.

Boy, was I wrong. Not only had he crawled out of the house, he was now making his way down our street. He had passed about four houses by the time I found him. To his credit, he was taking the sidewalk. And to the amusement of our neighbors, he was completely naked. It was quite a show for a lovely spring evening.

We later laughed at the consequences of that distraction, but not all our distracted moments are so comical. In fact, there is much for us to be concerned about as we consider the ongoing effects of technology on our families. Despite the increase of face time between children and parents, the quality of our engagement with one another is decreasing. As *The Atlantic* notes, the effects are problematic for both children and parents, and the future consequences are largely unknown:

> For all the talk about children's screen time, surprisingly little attention is paid to screen use by parents themselves, who now suffer from what the technology expert Linda Stone more than 20 years ago called "continuous partial attention." This condition is harming not just us, as Stone has argued; it is harming our children. The new parental-interaction style can interrupt an ancient emotional cueing system, whose hallmark is responsive communication, the basis of most human learning. We're in uncharted territory.[2]

But the problem isn't limited to relationships between kids and parents. It affects marriages as well. I recently saw a meme that said, "Marriage is just texting each other memes from different rooms." Sadly, while that's funny, it's also true for some people. More and more marriages are experiencing the negative consequences of our distracted lives. By one estimate, one-third of divorces in recent years were the result of people addicted to or wrongly interacting with Facebook.[3] Other studies are more conservative in their findings but still note a significant link between higher social media use and decreased marriage quality.[4] While more research needs to be done, the initial findings are not encouraging. Nor are they surprising.

DISTRACTION KNOWS NO AGE

I would imagine that your life is filled with distractions as well. That's probably why you picked up this book. And even that is ironic because one of the growing distractions in our world is the number of unread books on our bookshelves. Of the books I buy or am gifted by others, I may start one out of three and finish only one out of ten. If you're anything like me, the chances that you'll finish this book without getting distracted are about as good as the chances that I'll finish this chapter without checking my email.

Gimme a minute. I'll be right back.

I don't need to spend a lot of time telling you how distracted our world is. You already know that. There are more distractions today than there have ever been in the history of the world. Consider that we have a law that prohibits you from operating a motor vehicle while staring at your phone. That we even need this law is ludicrous, and it's a symptom of a deeper problem. For crying out loud, when you're operating a machine of moving metal, you should probably focus on what's ahead. I'm talking to myself at this point.

Before we blame the Millennials for another problem, I want to be clear this is *not* a generational thing, or a gender thing, or a temperament thing. Distraction—whether due to technology or simply the changing pace of life in our world— has affected all of us. It touches every part of our lives.

I see distracted Baby Boomers. A good friend of mine called just before Christmas and said, "My sixty-five-year-old parents are more distracted by their iPads than my five-year-old son. I honestly think I'm going to put restrictions on their devices while they're at my house for the next week." Let me know how that turned out, my friend.

I see it in the Gen Xers. I just read a study that said the age group most addicted to their phones is those middle-aged, "graying Gen Xers."[5] Not only is this generation of adults using their devices forty minutes more each day than their younger peers, they are the most likely to pull out their phones at the dinner table. Much of their device use is work related and commonly justified as necessary. "The midpoint of life is when your need to communicate peaks," Clive Thompson writes.[6] And that *need* to stay in touch with friends, keep up with the emails at work, and manage life can easily lead to habits of distraction.

Obviously, distraction is affecting the Millennial generation. I'm in that odd spot of having been born at the borderline of the Millennial years, so I'm sensitive to the glut of critique and criticism this generation has received. My Millennial coworkers are excited for Gen Z to take some of the spotlight now. They're ready to be left alone. Still, we can't turn a blind eye to the way the abundance of information in recent times has created countless more distractions than in previous generations. There was a day when you didn't know the answer to something and you simply didn't know. Millennials have grown up with the mantra: "Well, we don't have to *not* know!" And this awareness that somewhere out there the answer or that one bit of information can be found has created an unprecedented level of distraction. Consider all the options we have now . . . Google it or Shazam it or Wikipedia it or ask Alexa. But we no longer have to *not* know.

Side note: Whoever drew the line between Gen Xers and Millennials got it wrong. The real point of delineation between these two generations is the popularization of the internet. Growing up with an accessible internet means a radically different childhood from someone who didn't have that experience. I was born in 1980, and while I'm "technically" a borderline Millennial, it's absurd to compare my experience with that of someone born after the early '90s. If you remember the experience of pulling over to a gas station and frantically looking for a quarter to use a pay phone, you're not a Millennial.

And let's not forget the distractions in the Gen Z generation. A few months ago, I walked around a college campus for a few hours, and as I passed classroom after classroom, I was struck by how different they look today from when I was in college. Every student was staring at a laptop or a tablet or a phone. And if you were foolish enough to think they were taking notes, you'd be wrong, because they weren't. I don't think a single student was paying attention to the professor. And I don't blame them. I can't even imagine how much ADHD medication I would have needed as a college student if I'd had internet access sitting in a college physics class. Not a chance of paying attention.

I'm not writing this book to blame everything on the almighty smartphone, although it does belong square in the crosshairs as enemy number one. According to the most recent Global Mobile Consumer Survey taken by Deloitte, most people take their phones to the dinner table, watch TV with a device in front of them, sleep next to their phones, check their email first thing in the morning, and even wake up in the middle of the night to check it.[7] What's interesting is comparing the number of people who say their smartphone is a problem with the number of people who say they're actively doing something about it. Both are growing at staggering rates.

No, the actual phone or device is not the root of our problem. It's only the conduit to other things—programs and games and images that stimulate our minds and bodies and shape our thoughts and desires. All this simply exacerbates feelings of discontent and increases our longing to feed our unsatisfied desires and provide for unmet needs. As comedian Gary Gulman jokes, "The phone is just a seldom-used app on my phone."[8] It's every other app on the phone that is fighting for our attention and the attention of our children. I'm alarmed when I hear that many app developers don't allow their own kids to use the software they create. Steve Jobs himself was a low-tech parent.[9] I wonder what these people know that most of us are missing. Perhaps those closest to the problem in Silicon Valley see the danger for what it really is. In an article in the *New York Times*, Nellie Bowles writes, "The people who are closest to a thing are often the most wary of it. Technologists know how phones really work, and many have decided they don't want their own children anywhere near them."[10]

People are starting to wake up to the numbing effects of

our distracting technologies and the attention-grabbing noises and sights of our consumer culture. I'm distracted, you're distracted—we're all distracted—but those distractions are not the real problem. It's actually worse than that.

THE REAL PROBLEM WITH DISTRACTIONS

This world of distraction collects a toll from us. All the benefits of technology and our media-saturated, 24/7 consumer culture come at a cost. And it may be more expensive than you realize. I'm not talking about the sum of your music, media, and food subscriptions (though you may want to add the total of your Stitch Fix, Dollar Shave Club, Amazon Prime, Hulu, HBO Go, Evernote Premium, and Blue Apron monthly fees sometime). Dave Ramsey would certainly be pleased if you did the math on that, but I'm referring to something deeper than mere dollars and cents. All these distractions are costing you something that you can't see, at least not immediately. And you need to understand this cost, because living unaware would be a tragic mistake.

The distractions in my life have cost me something far greater than the nuisance of a stolen car. The Chattanooga PD eventually found my car, but one unexpected benefit of having it stolen that night was how it forced me to slow down from my normal crazy pace. I was able to step back and realize that my distracted lifestyle was not healthy or sustainable. Like most do-it-yourself home improvement projects, distractions will make the things you want to do in life take longer and cost more than you might realize. In the weeks that followed, I was able to identify several problems caused by distractions, and after categorizing and combining them, I've narrowed them down to three price tags you'll need to pay, if not now, then at some point in the future:

1. The opportunity cost of the unknown.
2. The lack of traction caused by the distraction.
3. The failure to live your best life.

Let's consider each of them as we get started.

The Opportunity Cost of the Unknown

First, let's think about what I call the *opportunity cost* of your distractions. I'm assuming you're familiar with this term. It alludes to the unknown nature of the things your distractions are distracting you from. When economists and sociologists talk about *opportunity costs*, they are speaking of the benefits you miss out on by choosing one thing over another. With all the benefits of technology, we tend to downplay or overlook some of those costs. But the truth is that with every notification alert, or every mouse click, or that "I'm gonna read just one more" Reddit strand, or whatever your current Netflix rabbit hole is, you are being distracted *from* something. That time, that energy, that moment where you are present—it's sacrificed and lost. An *opportunity* is lost with every distraction we feed.

What is that opportunity? Honestly, I don't know. And for your life right now, it doesn't matter whether *I* know. What matters is whether *you* know. I'll give you some examples if you're having a difficult time coming up with any. It might be the opportunity to develop stronger, more meaningful relationships. It might be the ability to be more present with those around you. It might be the opportunity to develop a skill you wouldn't otherwise develop. It might be a chance to become more emotionally aware. But whatever it is on the other side of that distraction, I know it's something worth discovering. But you won't gain the benefits of those opportunities because of the distractions in your life. Every opportunity lost has a cost.

The Lack of Traction Caused by the Distraction

If we do an etymology study on the word *distract*, it gives us a simple picture that can teach us something true about the opportunity cost of our distractions. The word *distract* means "to draw apart," and that definition is rooted in the two syllables that make up the word. The Latin verb *trahere* (-tract) means "to draw," and the prefix *dis* means "away from." Our distractions are literally drawing us away from something.

"Caw. Caw. Hey. Who. Who. Hey! You two. *You!* Lookuphere! Lookuphere!"[11] (Thank you, Lucky Day, as played by Steve Martin in *Three Amigos.*)

Okay, back to the word *distract*. Yes, to distract someone is to pull them away from something. Your distractions are pulling you away from other things, important things, things and people you love and goals you want to achieve. Your distractions are keeping you from gaining momentum in your life. They are keeping you from gaining *traction* in your life. Look closely at the word again.

Dis-*traction.*

A lack of traction in life will eventually lead to disaster. On Tuesday, January 28, 2014, Winter Storm Leon attacked Atlanta, Georgia, with two (yes, two) inches of snow, causing chaos that left Atlanta resembling a real-life scene from *The*

Walking Dead. A loss of traction caused the devastation and mayhem. When traction is lost, things that are in motion will spin out of control. They *have* nothing to grab hold of, nothing to allow for forward momentum. For your own quick distraction, do yourself a favor and Google "2014 Atlanta snowstorm" to see what I mean.

This was a day I'll never forget as Leon created a massive gridlock on the highways and interstates throughout the city; 1,254 car accidents were reported and thousands of cars were left stranded on the sides of roads. Atlanta mayor Kasim Reed defended his handling of the situation, arguing, "We got one million people out of the city of Atlanta in about 12 hours."[12] And he was right. There were countless reports of people experiencing 10-hour+ commutes home, many of them eventually abandoning their cars and walking the remainder of the way.

Over the next several weeks, the snowstorm was the number one topic of conversation with everyone I bumped into. And the most common question was, "How long did it take you to get home during Snowmageddon?" Everyone had their own story of walking several miles to get home, staying overnight at a friend's house, or even spending the night in the aisle of a CVS drugstore. All this chaos was caused by a single problem: the loss of traction on the roadways.

Without traction, we can't move forward. And what people experienced literally in their vehicles during the Atlanta Snowmageddon is something that happens every day in our lives. So many of us know the feeling of just spinning our wheels. A lot of energy is expended. We can hear the noise and smell something happening, but we aren't gaining any momentum. We aren't moving forward. So many people are looking to find their footing in life but just can't seem to find any traction.

Is that you? If so, you're not alone. I know the consequences of an overabundance of distractions and the way they make us feel stuck. As a pastor, I'm well aware of that frustrating feeling of spinning my wheels, only to get nowhere. Countless people are busy and fill their days with loads of activities, only to collapse in bed at night exhausted. And they wonder, *Did I accomplish anything meaningful today?* Distraction-filled days lead to traction-less lives.

The Failure to Live Your Best Life

Honestly, I'm over the phrase "I'm living my best life." Has it reached "kids doing the floss dance" annoying? Not quite, but it's close. (Don't act like you've never tried the floss dance in front of a mirror in the privacy of your own home.) Seriously though, I'm over it. One more Instagram pic of your friend's post-yoga workout, her parents' killer lake house dock, or her latest order of avocado toast with the hashtag #LivingMyBestLife and we'll both hit *Send* on some regrettable snarky comment. Whether you're over that phrase or not, hopefully we can both agree that "living your best life," if it means anything, means a life of fewer distractions, not more.

And that leads me to a simple observation: your distractions are holding you back from becoming a better you! They are getting in the way of your ability to grow as a person and as a leader. They are holding you back from exerting effort on your own improvement. The distractions in your life are pulling you away from the things that truly matter, keeping you from living a life of momentum, forward progress, and growth. And that means they will certainly, if they haven't already, hamper your ability to live your best life. That's what distractions are meant to do.

CLEAR EYES AND FULL HEARTS

It's no wonder our society is perhaps the most stressed, depressed, and anxious group of humans ever to walk the planet. Distractions are like eating Tide pods. Objectively, it makes no sense and you will sound crazy trying to explain it to your grandmother. After you've given in to a distraction and satisfied that urge, you won't even be glad you did it, but it is guaranteed to get you to stop thinking about whatever it was you *were* thinking about—most likely something important and meaningful. You might have a story to share. And you will certainly have something to upload to YouTube. But it's a fleeting pleasure, here for a moment and then gone. A life of distractions is a shallow life, a life lived without self-awareness. It's a life lived in constant anticipation of the next thing that will keep you from slowing down to listen to what's happening within.

Well, I'm not okay with any of it—the Tide pods or the distractions. The good news is that you can do something about this. And I'm here to help. I wrote this book as a guide, a manual on how to turn down the distractions in your life. But my primary focus isn't on better time management or a plan to end your addiction to social media. I'll have some ideas there, but other books offer tips and techniques to deal with those things. My hope in this book is to help you taste and see what's on the other side. I want you to see with clarity and longing for the better life available to you if you begin to turn down your distractions. I want you to see that it's worth the effort. But here is the key: you are the only one who can actually do something about this. You are in charge of your own life. You are the one who needs to lead, and it starts by leading yourself. You're the only one who can honestly judge your distractions, look at what they're costing you, and then do something about them.

Obviously, you won't be able to eliminate all distractions from your life. As we'll discuss in the next chapter, that wouldn't even be healthy. You can, however, *limit* the distractions so you can begin to gain traction on the path that reflects your true desires, the things that matter most. As a pastor and spiritual advisor to many people, I've seen this happen in countless lives, and I've experienced it on a personal level in my own life as well. I promise you—you can do it and it is worth it!

This book is about getting back on track in a world that will distract you right into the ditch.

CHAPTER 2

WHITE
NOISE

The barrage of distractions in our lives is nothing if not consistent. Distractions manage to do two things really well. First, they make us promises. Yes, some distractions annoy and bother us, but most of the time we are able to ignore or decline them in favor of what we want. The distractions I want to focus on fall into another category. These are the distractions that offer us something we want—at least in that moment. They promise us something that we find pleasurable or that helps us cope through a difficult challenge.

Second, they deliver on their promises. And unlike the classic Ja Rule and Ashanti song, they are both *always* there when you call and *always* on time. You can bank on the fact that distractions will always be there, doing exactly what they say they will do.

Distractions make good on their promises even when those promises are quite empty. They may succeed at gaining our attention or demanding that we listen or look, but most of the time they don't have much substance to them. The promise behind many of the distractions in our lives is simple: If you pay attention to me, I promise you'll stop thinking about whatever you were thinking about. Again, that's what distractions do. They take your mind off whatever your mind was focused on. And that's about all they have to offer. They don't necessarily give you something better to think about or focus on. They don't make you better. They don't lead you somewhere inten-

Distractions don't make you better.

tionally. They're quick fixes, short-term solutions for momentary escapes from this life.

Not every distraction is bad or wrong. Many of them are helpful in a limited way. The truth is that we often cannot focus intently on serious matters every moment of every day. Sometimes we need a break. The simple definition of a distraction is "something that prevents someone from giving full attention to something else."[1] Obviously, many things fall under that category of "something else." And while many unproductive things distract us from important matters, some wonderful things we give our attention to keep us from giving our full attention to something else. Here are some examples of what I mean by a positive distraction:

- A thirst for learning that keeps talk radio on all the time.
- A desire to be healthy and fit that keeps you fascinated with your health.
- A drive to achieve that keeps you working hard.

Do you see what I mean? None of these distractions are bad, but they all have the potential to be dangerous. Why? Because they do just what they were designed to do. When we give our attention to anything, it will draw us away from something else. And that means that even good things like wanting to learn or wanting to be healthy can become distractions. It all depends on what you actually *need* to be focused on right now. And therein lies the great problem in defining a "distraction." Anything can be a distraction if it keeps us from the things we most need in order to be healthy and purposeful in every dimension of life. And this means that even good things can become problems. What all distractions have in common is their ability to mask or hide those deeper needs. Distractions keep us from focusing on what's really driving us: the desires, emotions, motives, and needs that lie beneath the surface.

A NEED FOR SLEEP

My wife and I are huge fans of white noise. And we love noise machines. Specifically, I support *heavy rain pouring, blowing wind*, and *brown noise*. Those are far and away the best forms of soothing noise for getting optimal sleep. Whenever the topic comes up with friends, I ask what they enjoy. Finding someone who likes an obscure noise like *frogs at night* always surprises me. I can't understand why someone would want to sleep with the noise of multiple frogs in a room. Maybe it's just me, but it seems absurd. It's not that I hate frogs. And I'm certainly not afraid of frogs. I just don't get along with frogs—especially in my bed.

Oh, that's irrational, Clay. Grow up.

No, it's not irrational. A few months ago, I was leaving the house early in the morning like I normally do. It was dark, and as I stepped onto our back deck, a frog jumped from out of nowhere and landed right on me. Yeah. Right on me. That is *not* cool. I felt attacked. And ever since then, I've existed in an undeclared war on amphibians in general. We had an arrangement that worked. We would simply leave each other alone. But clearly there was a misunderstanding somewhere, and I'm still not over it.

So sleeping with the sound of a chorus of frogs echoing throughout my room seems borderline crazy.

Anyway, back to this idea of white noise.

I love the concept of white noise. And one big reason is because we have five little kids and my wife and I have to have white noise to sleep. We actually cannot sleep without it. And we've trained our kids the same way. It's pretty cute when our two-year-old calls me back into the room with a frantic scream, only to let me know with the cutest lisp, "Daddy, you didn't turn on my *shound* machine." Please don't ever grow up.

You might ask, "But, Clay, with so much white noise, aren't you worried that something might happen at night that you won't hear?" Great question. Absolutely not. Because that's actually the point. I don't *want* to be awakened by a random cough or a kid who talks in his sleep or someone who needs a sip of water in the middle of the night.

White noise is an effective sound-masking tool. It creates a hum of soothing distraction to cover up the sounds you don't want to hear. It's commonly used in medical offices, counseling centers, and schools. In our office building, we pipe in white noise because the people working in cubicles need to have private conversations, sometimes with our pastors. When private conversations need to stay private and the walls or dividers are not thick enough to contain them, a little white noise goes a long way in helping mask what people are saying so it stays confidential. The constant low hum of the white noise is almost imperceptible, but it does what it's intended to do. It *masks* the noises we don't want to hear or don't want others to hear.

White noise has been a helpful metaphor for me to better grasp the power and the danger of distractions. As I'm writing this chapter, I'm sitting on an airplane trying to focus my thoughts even as myriad random sounds surround me. There are sniffles, coughs, a baby's cries, and a pilot randomly telling us that he's enjoying his morning. These are all distractions that I don't need right now. The white noise of music playing through my headphones is a strategic choice providing the necessary masking of sounds I don't want to hear.

Think about that. I use *noise* to mask the things that distract me.

Something important underlies this approach to dealing with distractions. And in a larger sense, I believe most of us are using some form of white noise to deal with the distractions in our lives. Just as my wife and I rely on our white noise machine to get a good night's sleep, this world of distraction we live in is filled with people masking and coping—all to experience some small measure of peace and rest.

Unfortunately, this solution—while effective—can lead to an even deeper problem.

TOO MUCH SOUND OR NO SOUND AT ALL

We utilize some form of white noise every day. It's all around us. And I'm not speaking of the literal noise of a machine; I'm thinking of the multitude of things we do to avoid the assault of distractions in our lives. Here are three things that are almost always true about the white noise in our lives:

1. It's masking something.
2. It's constant.
3. It's imperceptible.

Wherever you are right now, stop and try this little experiment. Humor me. Try to get in a place where it's as quiet as possible. Scientists tell us that most people consider 30 decibels a comfortably quiet level. Sit still and pay attention to what you can hear. I'll guarantee that you will still hear something, whether it's the hum of the air conditioner, the traffic outside, the birds chirping, or the breeze blowing through the trees. Some noise is always in our lives. Sometimes it's relatively quiet; other times it's blaring loud and obnoxiously. But there is always something for us to hear. It's impossible for us to live life without any noise. In fact, human beings have difficulty existing when the noise is completely gone. So you may not want to turn it *all* the way down.

The quietest room in the world is at Orfield Labs in Minneapolis, and it's so quiet that the only things you'll hear are your organs doing their thing—your heart beating, your lungs breathing. If you stay long enough in this anechoic chamber, it's possible the depth of silence might cause you to start hallucinating. The longest amount of time anyone has spent in the room is forty-five minutes. This form of solitary confinement is powerful enough to break the strongest of men,[2] even Lincoln Burrows from *Prison Break*.

If human beings need some noise in their lives to function in a healthy way, the question becomes: How much is healthy, and how much is too much? That's one reason white noise fascinates me. Turn it down too low and you'll start plucking out your eyebrows as every other distracting noise is amplified. But never turn it down and you might miss something that really *needs* your attention. If my wife and I have our noise machine cranked up too loud at night, we might never awaken to the smoke alarm or the cries of a child in a genuine emergency. As helpful as the white noise can be, it is indiscriminate, blocking *all* noises, even the ones we might want to hear.

And that's another thing you need to know about white noise: this noise is constant—it's always there. And it's imperceptible—if you don't stop to pay attention to it, you'll never notice it. That's what makes it so effective at masking.

An older, once popular song may help us better understand this reality. I appreciate how the band from Columbus, Ohio, Twenty One Pilots, described it in their song "Car Radio." I can't turn this book into a musical greeting card without jacking up the price, so without music the lyrics will read like a badly written teenage love poem, but they pack a pretty powerful punch when you listen. Try searching for the song on YouTube for a listen.

The storyline behind the song is that a guy has had his radio stolen from his car and is now all stuck in his head because the noise he used to have while driving is gone. The silence he experiences every time he drives forces him to wrestle with the fears that have lain dormant inside him all this time. He's seeing how the noise of the radio has masked them, but now admits: *"This time there's no sound to hide behind."* Now, in the silence, he's thinking thoughts he's tried to ignore: *"Oh dear, I don't know if we know why we're here."* And in the end, he's not comfortable without the noise. He wants the masking effect of the music to help him stop thinking about the deeper questions he wants to avoid: *"Oh my, too deep, please stop thinking, I liked it better when my car had sound."*

I love the simple power of music to reveal truth. And I hope you have begun to see that my real interest in this book is not to give you tips for silencing the notifications on your phone or suggestions for streamlining your schedule to be more productive. Good books have been written and are still being written that can help you set boundaries on your use of technology and media.

This book is about something else, something under and behind all that. It is about the "noise" in your life—the things you are doing to mask your deeper desires and emotions. In the Twenty One Pilots song, the radio served that purpose, masking the underlying fear that this man felt inside. But our masking tools aren't only music and media. As we've seen with our distractions, our masking tools can be good things that keep us from the most important things in life. The specifics will be unique to you, but what's not unique to any of us is this temptation to mask what's going on inside us.

That's what this book is really all about. The real danger of living in a world of constant distractions is not the distractions themselves. It's the things we use to block them out—because our attempts to mask and hide can keep us from knowing who we really are. This world is filled with people who have become adept at using white noise to lead successful lives.

But when that noise is gone, they find they are alone with a stranger. They don't know who they are, why they do what they do, or, most importantly, why they feel how they feel.

AUTOMATIC VOLUME CONTROL

What you might not realize is that you have control over all this. You have your fingers on the knob of that white noise machine in your life. We all do. When your circumstances are stressful and you face constant distraction, you're tempted to turn up the volume. When anxiety hits, you crank it up. When fear starts to surface, the easiest thing to do is to look to the noise to help. The noise masks whatever it is you don't want to feel. This temptation to turn up the noise has become so deeply ingrained in us, it's hardly a conscious decision. It has become automatic.

What we need is a growing self-awareness. For you to develop into the leader you want to be, for you to be the friend, spouse, or coworker who is a healthy influence on those around you, you must learn to pay attention to that volume knob.

A few years ago, car manufacturers started integrating automatic volume control (AVC) as a feature to keep a constant signal-to-noise ratio inside a car. Whether or not your car has this feature, you've probably had the experience of being in a car that leverages AVC. It's pretty fantastic. When the car is wide open on the highway or you're driving along on the interstate, the volume of the stereo increases. Likewise, when you pull up to a traffic light, the volume in the car turns down. The automatic volume control adjusts based on the noises around you.

If you fail to pay attention, you'll find that you've been

You have your fingers on the knob of that white noise machine in your life.

conditioned to do the same thing on a moment-by-moment basis. When the stress or fear inside you is particularly strong, you'll naturally turn up the volume on the noise around you. What does that look like? For some, you'll be more likely to check social media, find a season to binge on Netflix, or, worse, turn to more dangerous forms of noise. Because of the abundance of distractions in the world today, when we start to sense that something isn't right or our underlying emotional needs aren't being met 100 percent, we're hardwired to use automatic volume control.

FINDING YOUR VOLUME KNOB

We all have our own white noises—a variety of coping mechanisms we use to block out distractions in our lives. But that white noise also blocks out the emotions we'd prefer not to feel. And that can be dangerous . . . and unhealthy. When we feel overwhelmed, afraid, depressed, or discouraged, we turn up the dial on our white noise. Not only does it help us avoid the outward distractions, it mutes the inner voice telling us how we're doing.

Until my college years, school came pretty easy. I'd pay attention in class, get together with some friends to study for tests, do a few problems, write a few sentences, and get by with As and Bs. But college was another story. I was majoring in industrial engineering, and it didn't take me long to realize I was way out of my league. I should have changed to a different major that was a better fit for my personality and skill set, but I was too stubborn to change.

Near the end of my time at Georgia Tech, I was having

trouble meeting the matriculation requirements. I was struggling to master a few classes. I like to say I decided to take them a few times . . . just to make sure I really understood the material. At this point, I knew I wasn't going to be pursuing a career in engineering, as I was planning to attend graduate school to study theology, so I set up a meeting with the registrar to see if she would allow me to skip some classes I wanted to avoid.

I'll never forget that meeting. I immediately learned that she was a cat lady. She really, really loved cats. Do you know any cat ladies? They always fascinate me because it takes a certain kind of person to strike a strong connection with felines. This woman had pictures of cats all over her office.

I decided to get right to the point.

"Ma'am, I'm going to be honest with you. I'm not even seeking employment in the engineering field, because I'm headed to graduate school to study theology. Let's make a deal on this engineering degree. If you promise to give it to me, I'll promise never to use it."

It was a good day. She obliged.

My time at Georgia Tech was challenging, but I was determined to get through it. And, unfortunately, that is exactly what I did. During those years, I shut down and focused so I could do what I needed to do and get out. And I was not the only one. I've noticed that alumni of Georgia Tech don't ask, "When did you *graduate?*" They say, "When did you *get out?*" It's a challenging school for most students. And it just about did me in.

Studying was always a struggle because it unearthed emotions I would have rather avoided. As I'd sit down to review something, I was like Drake, all up in my feelings. "Keke, do you love me?"

I always felt incompetent. Inferior. Inadequate.

And so all through those years, I tried to focus, removing the distractions both externally and internally by keeping my fingers on the dial, ready to turn up the white noise when it was needed.

- I'd text a bunch of friends to see what else was going on.
- I'd reformat my desktop computer.
- I'd organize my calendar.
- I'd balance my checkbook (remember that blast from the past?).

Honestly, I'd do anything to take my mind off how studying made me *feel*. I wanted something to mask what was happening inside me, so I'd look for some noise to mute it to a manageable level.

When something we don't like is screaming *inside* us, we always find something *outside*—an external distraction—and turn it up. And it works. That outside noise distracts us for a time. It mutes the inner turmoil, the uncomfortable emotions, the pain, the inadequacy, the discomfort, the memories. It hides whatever we don't want to feel or experience.

And there are more options for white noise today than ever before.

My time at Georgia Tech was just before our current age of social media. Wi-Fi was being installed in our buildings, and we were still a few years from having smartphones. At that time, you could find a quiet place in the library and avoid distractions. But today things are different. Now the distractions are always with us. And the white noise we use to mask how we are feeling is there as well. There's more noise today than ever before. And it's only growing louder.

THE DANGER OF THE NOISE

Can we agree that the distraction of white noise is causing a problem? I sure hope so. And if so, maybe you're asking, "Well, what are the implications of being overly distracted and consistently failing to pay attention to those important things inside us that are screaming for our attention?"

Great question, my friend. So glad you asked. Let me first give you a random anecdote that recently caught my attention, because I think it will show what might happen if we played out this scenario.

In the fall of 2016, America's collective jaw dropped to the floor at the results of the presidential election. Almost all the preliminary polls had slated Hillary Rodham Clinton to come out victorious over Donald J. Trump, but the surprising results left both ends of the political spectrum shocked. Many people were thrilled and many others were absolutely devastated. Clearly, so as not to risk losing you for the rest of this book, I'm not about to drop a political endorsement or make some political commentary.

In the days that followed, I remember reading headlines like this one: **"Professors Cancel Class, Responding to 'Shocking' Election Results."**

I'm sorry, what? This made no sense to me. What do the results of the election have to do with my looming physics exam? Here's an excerpt:

Responding to Donald Trump's shocking presidential victory, several Cornell professors across departments cancelled class Wednesday, citing personal distress and concern for students' emotional well-being.

Professor Jane-Marie Law, Asian, Near Eastern, and religious studies, said she cancelled her "Introduction to Japan and Religion" lecture, because she was "so upset and worried I would break down, thinking about how dangerous the move the American electorate—half of them—made last night is."[3]

Now, I don't want to make light of the emotional anguish caused by the results of the election for many students and professors. Everyone was shocked and not everyone was at peace about the results. But I couldn't understand what the results of an election had to do with canceling classes. That's not how things worked for me in college. If I had emailed a college professor to say, "I don't think I'm in a place to take that test tomorrow because I'm overwhelmed with my emotions—I'm just not *feeling* it," they would not have been sympathetic. Almost certainly, I would have received a response like this, "Mr. Scroggins, I'm so sorry about your *feelings*. We are going to have the test tomorrow, and if you don't take it, I'm not *feeling* like you will pass this class."

Maybe the election results are the exception to the norm. But I worry that a response like canceling classes is more likely an indication of how we're teaching emerging adults to deal with their feelings and emotions. Is it good to know how you feel? Of course! But does that mean our emotions should control our lives? I recently spoke with an emerging adult who told me, "I've never learned how to deal with my emotions. In my teenage years, I ate my feelings. In college, I drank my feelings away. Now I'm in my twenties and I've cried until my eyes are red and raw because I don't know what to do with them."

Between the two extremes of masking emotions, as I did at Georgia Tech, and letting our emotions run wild so that they control our lives, there is a healthy way of listening to what's happening and leading ourselves forward.

If we think the answer to our emotions is to cancel class, run to social media, or use masking tools to avoid what's inside, it's no wonder we're getting the results we're seeing. As one of my mentors likes to say, "Your system is perfectly designed for the results you're getting."[4]

EVERYONE GETS A TROPHY

When I was a kid, I was inundated with affirmation and encouragement. Participation trophies were just rising in popularity as I was hitting my teenage years. And the trickle of self-affirmation mantras was picking up speed.

Just do it.

Aim for the moon. If you miss, you'll land in the stars.

The best gift you can give the world is yourself.

Unfortunately, these positive affirmations were not enough. Even words of affirmation can be a masking tool, keeping us from facing the truth about ourselves. If affirmation is not both loving *and* honest, it can leave us feeling worse on the inside. With all the positive messages we've given our children, you would think our world would be filled with secure, confident, and healthy adults. Not quite. Instead, our world is filled with adults brimming with confidence and crippled by insecurity.

Positive affirmation can be another form of white noise. It mutes and masks what is true and can even prevent us from looking honestly at ourselves. We learn to affirm without evaluating. Like turning up the white noise machine while the fire alarm is telling you the house is burning down around you, it's a dangerous habit. "Self-affirmation—apart from self-evaluation—is the beginning of self-deception and the end of self-development."[5]

If we affirm ourselves without evaluating ourselves honestly and in depth, we end up smuggling our unprocessed emotions into the future. Anytime we fail to process our emotions, they fester. The very thing that attracts us to white noise—the ability to mute and mask the emotions we don't want to face—can lead us to habits of avoidance that end up paralyzing us and stunting our emotional growth. When you don't want to deal with what's inside you, you'll turn up the volume knob so the noise around you is louder

> Either you'll learn to handle your emotions or your emotions will end up handling you.

and louder. Either you'll learn to handle your emotions or your emotions will end up handling you.

Turn Down for What?

Your emotions are too important to stuff down, avoid, or deny. And it's all too likely you and I are doing this in some form at this very moment. The longer those emotions lie unattended to, the more devastating their consequences. Becoming a healthy person demands that you deal with them. And you can only deal with them if you're aware that they exist.

Since 2014, the chart-topping song "Turn Down for What" could be heard in every club, every locker room, every dorm, and in my car on repeat. DJ Snake and Lil John confront us with an existential question of the highest order, asking if anything should cause us to not turn up. For Snake and Lil John, "turning up" means more than simply showing up. It means showing up with energy, passion, and drip (thanks, Migos).

I'm all for turning things up. I agree—we need people who are ready to lead with passion, who aren't going to back down or hide. But I hope you see that it's not enough to crank up the noise in your life. We aren't looking for more enthusiasm or people who are going to try harder. We don't want to mask what's going on inside.

So the answer isn't turning things up. Before we can lead with passion, we need to turn the noise down. We need to find space and quiet to learn how to listen—to hear what's being said inside us, where there is pain, where there are fears, where there are dreams and hopes that we've never said out loud.

Being a better version of you demands that you turn down the noise. The future you, your future spouse, your future kids, the future people you hope to lead—they all demand that you turn down the noise.

Let me make it as simple as possible. Here are three steps to turning down the noise in your life:

1. Name your noise.
2. Experiment with your noise.
3. Listen to what's there.

Name Your Noise

As I've shared these concepts with emerging leaders and different organizations, I've asked thousands of people to name the most common forms of white noise in their lives. I'm always amazed how similar the answers are, regardless of the audience. Whether the crowd is a group of business leaders, church leaders, parents of teenagers, or even college students, the most common answers are the same:

- Work
- Television
- Radio
- News
- Podcasts
- Exercise
- Alcohol
- Eating
- Shopping

The list goes on and on. I offer these as a starting point to spark some thinking about your own life. Can you identify your most common form of noise? The truth is, each of us has our fingers on the volume knob. We all have something we use to mask the distractions in our lives, both externally and internally. What is that white noise for you? What do you use to avoid the distractions, that white noise that seems to help and may even offer you the promise of a good night's rest, but is also hindering you from hearing the other sounds you need to hear right now? Until you identify it, you can't turn it down.

Some forms of noise are even more specific to those who

identify as leaders. In the next chapter, we'll look at three of the most common distractions in leadership and how leaders use white noise in their lives to avoid these distractions. But for now, I want you to picture your fingers on that volume knob. Think of what you do when life is crazy and the distractions are overwhelming you. What does it look like for you when you turn up that noise? Or think of it this way: What is masking the voice inside your head? What is silencing your inner voice?

Experiment with Your Noise

Observe. Hypothesize. Change a variable. Test. Repeat.

The process I just summarized is known as the scientific method. And while I first learned it in my science classes, over the years I've grown to love it as a method for learning in all of life. Even though Francis Bacon is widely considered the author of this method, many others like Copernicus, Galileo, and Newton followed this process and in doing so have greatly shaped the way we discover and learn.

Whether you realize it or not, you probably use the scientific method every day.

Observe: *My lamp isn't working.*

Hypothesize: *It should work.*

Change a variable: *I'll plug it into a different socket to test the power.*

Test: *Let's turn it on, and if that doesn't work, let's try another socket.*

Observe: *It still doesn't work.*

Self-leadership demands that you know more about yourself than anyone else. You need a PhD in you, and in order to become well versed in the ins and outs of yourself, you need to observe and understand the distractions and noises in your life. You need to learn to employ the scientific method.

My wife is a master at this. She knows herself well and is always learning more, growing in self-awareness. When we were dating, I was pretty sure she was a better person than me, but now, after twelve years of marriage, I'm thoroughly convinced it's true—and much of that is due to the work she has done to know and understand herself. At the start of each month, she practices a discipline in which she chooses something and temporarily stops doing it for that month. She pauses, observes the things she is currently doing, decides whether she can stop doing something, and then changes that variable. She cuts it out. She quits it. She's experimenting with the noise.

Self-leadership demands that you know more about yourself than anyone else.

What might it look like to stop making personal purchases for a month, whether new pillows for the couch or another hoodie sweatshirt or one more book you'll probably never read? What if I went without dessert for a month? She knows herself well enough to understand that she will never have the answer to that question unless she forces herself to try it. It's quite simple. Turn down the noise, remove the masking mechanism, and listen to what's there when it's gone.

At the beginning of the month, she makes her pick, and she always asks me if I want to play along. Nine times out of ten, I say, "No thanks." And without any judgment, she goes ahead with her experiment, proving that she is the better person in our marriage.

So what about you? What can you experiment with? Are we friends enough for me to ask you a few questions?

1. What feels like it has become a habit for you?
2. What would others say has become a distraction for you?
3. When you're stressed, anxious, fearful, or apathetic, where do you go—what do you do—to escape those feelings?

Your greatest sources of noise pollution are found near the answers to those questions. If you're having trouble figuring these out, ask someone else. I guarantee that your kids, your roommates, your coworkers, and your #bae all have a pretty good idea of what those things might be. If you still can't think of anything, try these:

- Put your phone in a drawer for an hour a day.
- Don't touch your computer on a Sunday.
- Go for a week without doing any personal internet shopping.

If you find these initial attempts helpful, you can advance to the ninja level like my wife and try quitting something for an entire month. But you may not be able to start there.

Here's the thing: *you don't have to quit it forever.* I'm only asking you to name it and turn it down for a season. Observe. Hypothesize. Change a variable. Test. Repeat.

Listen to What's There

There's a why behind all this. It's not simply a random exercise. You're learning to identify what your particular white noise might be, but there's more to it than that. You're taking baby steps toward teaching yourself how to be a student of yourself. You're learning how to self-evaluate.

One of my favorite graduate school professors was Dr. Howard Hendricks, who used to say all the time, "Experience alone isn't helpful. Evaluated experience is what's helpful." When you turn down the noise low enough and long enough, you give yourself the gift of quiet. And in that quiet, you need to listen.

Your emotions are messengers. They're trying to tell you something.

This past Halloween, my wife told me she was going to take a break from all social media for the month of November, and something inside me said, *You should probably do that too.* So I did. And during that month, I learned a few things about myself.

First, I learned that I do have the power to say no. This was huge. And maybe it's something you need to experience as well. I don't consider myself someone with a lot of self-control or willpower. But before we can change something, we must believe it's *possible* to change. As silly as it might sound, the positive feelings I experienced from going without social media for a month were encouraging to me. Those positive emotions reinforced my sense of commitment and showed me that I could pick a goal, stick to the goal, and achieve the goal. This realization in itself helped me see that some negative emotions had already hardened into beliefs. I learned I was subconsciously believing lies that told me I wasn't capable or disciplined enough to quit a habit. The simple act of trying it for a month showed me that I could choose to be disciplined. Don't miss that. It all begins with that first step.

Second, I realized social media was exhausting me. This was one of the more surprising things I learned. Taking a month away from something I had done every day, multiple times a day, made me realize how exhausting it had become. It was draining my energy, leaving me mentally, emotionally, and even physically fatigued. About a week into November, my wife and I agreed that we weren't missing it. It didn't feel like a sacrifice. We actually enjoyed being away from social media. I hadn't consciously grasped the subtle pressure I had felt to post about my life and keep up with the appearance of activity until I wasn't doing it every day. I didn't know how refreshing it was not to feel that. Of course, the constant temptation to compare ourselves to other people is still very real. Getting off social media doesn't make that go away. If anything, it helped me see how much of my time and energy had been in service to that desire. And though getting away diminished the temptation, I know it was still there—and this led to my third discovery.

Third, I realized that social media was not the problem. Sure, it's *a* problem, but it's not *the* problem. If you had asked me before taking this break what the white noise was in my life, I might have mentioned being addicted to aimlessly scrolling through Instagram and Twitter. But it turns out that my perceived addiction to social media wasn't as bad as I thought it was. Quitting wasn't that hard.

But that opened my eyes to my real problem. You see, I

took the time I wasn't spending on social media and used it to do other things on my phone.

- I checked the weather way more often. *Interesting. Tomorrow has a higher dew point.*
- I randomly shopped online more often. *Oh wow. Costco has Instapots on sale!*
- I read more articles on my browser. *"600 Surfing Santas Make a Big Splash in Cocoa Beach."*[6] (That was actually a true story.)

The problem was that I was removing one form of white noise but replacing it with another. The good news was that I was one step closer to understanding this and now could do something about it.

This was a simple exercise, something anyone can do. And while it won't change your life, it's a step in the right direction. Remember, you have emotions inside you that will not be addressed until you're aware of them. And you can't be aware of them if the noise in your life is so loud that you can't hear them. So you need to start somewhere. Pick something—some white noise that you are using to mask the distractions in your life, internally and externally. Turn it down. Then listen to what's there.

Plato once said, "An unexamined life is not worth living." I'm not sure I'd go that far. I think life is still pretty good even if we aren't always 100 percent self-aware. But I'd agree with the overall idea and say that, while an unexamined life might still be worth living, if we don't examine our lives, we'll never experience anything better than what we have now. There's no hope for things to get better and, most likely, they will get worse over time. And that's flat-out discouraging. To examine your life, you must learn to name your noise, experiment with turning down the volume, and then listen to what's left in the quiet that follows.

TOO MUCH LIGHT

Here's a sad statistic. At least 55 percent of the population of the UK cannot see the Milky Way when they look up at the night sky.[7] Their lovely British cities create so much light that the gorgeous collection of stars is virtually invisible to more than half the people living there. This could have been terribly tragic a generation ago. John, Paul, George, and Ringo would have totally missed "Lucy in the Sky with Diamonds" if they were writing songs today.

Light pollution occurs when a high level of excess, human-originated light fundamentally alters natural conditions.[8] Light pollution has been said to compromise health, disrupt ecosystems, and spoil aesthetic environments (like viewing the Milky Way in the UK). In places where too much light is produced at night, we lose the opportunity to see the natural light the stars provide.

Contrast this with my first visit to Wyoming. I will never forget looking up at the clear night sky, away from cities and human lights, to really see the natural light of the stars for the first time in my life. Astronomy has never been something I've thought much about, but that spectacular show left an indelible impression on me. Like the time I first visited the Amish countryside of Pennsylvania, I couldn't stop staring. The stars that night were otherworldly. I had been blinded by inferior lights and had never experienced something so wonderfully and astonishingly bright.

So here's my dumb question for you. *Are the stars in Wyoming actually any brighter than the stars you might see in New York, Beijing, or Mexico City?* Of course not. They are the same stars with the same light traveling millions of light-years to reach our eyes. But they appear brighter to you and me when the pollution—the interference—of other lights is diminished. In places with little to no light pollution, such as Sedona, Arizona, or Fort Davis, Texas, or Lake Powell, Utah, the stars aren't shining any brighter; it's simply that you and I can finally see them as they really are.

When you remove the distortion other light creates, the stars seem to shine brighter. Remove the distortion to see more clearly. Quiet the noise to gain clarity.

In the next chapter, we'll continue learning how to turn down the noise by identifying it and naming it. And in particular, we'll look at what this means for leaders. Leaders have unique distractions that fight for our attention, our focus, and our energy. And if we're not careful, the very thing we need to see might be right in front of us, but we're simply too blind to see it.

CHAPTER SUMMARY

1. As feelings surface, you will be tempted to turn up some form of noise to avoid dealing with them.
2. Turning up the noise will keep you from dealing with what's inside you.

3. The longer and louder the noise, the more your feelings remain unattended to.

4. Avoiding your feelings stunts your emotional growth. Emotional avoidance is costly and complicated.

5. Turning down the noise involves naming your noise, experimenting with it, and listening to what's there.

CHAPTER 3

THE THREE
VILLAINS
OF
LEADERSHIP

Leadership involves an internal versus external dynamic. We've looked at the temptation all of us face to mask or hide the things that distract us using different forms of white noise. And one of the problems with white noise—our default coping techniques—is that when we turn up the noise, we risk losing the ability to hear what's happening inside. Understanding this internal versus external dynamic is key to becoming a leader who leads through, and not in reaction to, our distractions. Leadership would be a piece of cake for most of us were it not for those external factors we first have to navigate around. Captain Obvious strikes again!

The danger is that leadership can easily turn into a constant battle with external factors. Budgets. Calendar. Employees. Bosses. Market forces and trends. Technological change. Family. Bills. Public opinion. I mean, think about what takes up most of your working day. You sit in meeting after meeting to solve problems or plan for eventualities. You work at a sprint to hit a deadline. You restrategize your marketing based on a new competitor in your sector—and on and on to lead through the unpredictability of external factors.

Good leaders learn to manage external factors well. A good leader can respond effectively to even the most abrupt external changes. But here's the kicker: great leaders do so much more than this. They learn to focus intently on the internal factors only they can control. Leaders who stand out from the rest have learned to tune out the distraction of external factors, not by using white noise, but in a way that enables them to focus better on what's going on inside. It's not the glamorous work of breaking boards or slicing through chunks of ice, but it's the stuff that makes great leaders.

If you take a second to think about the internal forces that lay within your control waiting to be harnessed and put to good use, you'll find the most powerful of them all is your mind, your ability to think. I'm not talking about the power of positive thinking; I'm talking about the power of creating a specific vision for your future.

Andy Stanley describes vision as "your *preferred* future." If you and I were sitting across from one another having a drink and I asked you, "What does your preferred future look like?" how would you answer? Some of us have the answer locked and loaded. We've been quietly daydreaming about it since we first sat in an office cubicle. But others of us have barely thought about it in any great detail. And it's not because you don't care, because I know you do. So why is it? I think it's because we've spent the majority of our mental energy responding to the noise and distraction of the present moment. It makes sense. There's so much of it.

But when you constantly live in *present mind*, you'll continue to operate in *present mode*, and the next few years won't look much different than the last few—regardless of your level of output. That's a recipe for extreme frustration. I promise you, painting a picture of your preferred future is worth every minute you spend on it. It might be worthwhile to take some time to sit down with a piece of paper and sketch out some details of your personal vision. Bullet-point it. Spend some time asking yourself what you want your future career to look like; consider the level of financial freedom you hope to achieve in the future; think about the kind of relational health you'd like to develop. There's something powerful about unleashing your imagination on these sorts of questions. And when you do, you shift from *present mind* to *future mind* and catapult into *future mode*.

In 1937 Napoleon Hill published the bestselling book *Think and Grow Rich*. While Hill could be a somewhat shady character at times, there's good reason his book proved to be wildly popular and inspirational to so many. After spending time with some of the wealthiest and most successful people of the time, and having intermittently achieved some success of his own, he took time to examine the patterns of success. And what he found was that people who experienced extreme personal growth and improvement maintained fervid expectations for their future.

In other words, when people had an outrageously positive vision for their preferred future self, they tended to *become* what they *envisioned*.

Envision your future self. That's the first step toward seeing that person show up in your future. Even better, if you can learn to turn down the noise and tune out the distractions long enough, you might start to see that person showing up in the present.

THE AXIS OF DISTRACTION

Let's start getting specific about these distractions, shall we? If they're worth eliminating, they're worth naming.

While there are innumerable external pressures and sources of distraction in our lives and leadership, three in particular stand out. These are the three distractions that have the strongest gravitational pull on leaders' attention. I've definitely had to wrestle with these more than others. Together, I call them the *Axis of Distraction*.

The first one's a doozy, because it's so deceptive. This form of distraction wants you to believe it is the whole point of leadership and not a distraction from it. It wants you to believe it's the goal, not a byproduct. It wants you to see it as the end in itself, instead of the midway point that it is.

It's the *appearance of success*.

At this point I can hear you asking, "Clay, shouldn't we want to be successful? Isn't that what we've been talking about in this chapter—working on the small things that lead to success?" And you're right. I do want you to be successful. Heck, I want to be successful. We all do. And we should. But the first member of this unholy trinity of distraction is not *being successful*; rather, it's the *appearance of success*.

Have you ever shopped online for home furnishings? If you

have, you'll have spent some time scrolling through endless pictures of lamps, rugs, and seating choices for every occasion. I love buying things online. The convenience of clicking a button and having a couch show up at my front door a few days later brings a level of satisfaction the ancients never could have imagined. But what the ancients never had to deal with was the stress of judging the quality of a couch fabric from an array of souped-up pictures online. I've purchased things that on my computer screen looked like they were covered in high-quality leather and I imagined them smelling like intelligence and royalty. A few days later, the real thing showed up smelling like bad decisions and spilled gasoline fumes from some grimy warehouse.

Some things look great until you get up close and take another look. Sometimes silver is actually just sexy tinfoil. *Not everything that glitters is gold.*

And so it is with success.

Sometimes, underneath the appearance of success you'll find someone stumbling toward mediocrity or even on a path toward failure. But our hunger for the *appearance* of success has earned fortunes for people with large social media platforms. People love to present the best version of themselves on apps like Instagram. I'm betting you've watched an Instagram story or two that showed a couple madly in love, but you knew that behind the scenes their relationship wasn't all candy and roses. There are times when those legs tanning on the beach are just a pair of frankfurters in front of a tropical screensaver. We all know this, yet people still pour hours of their day into getting those pictures just right, throwing the perfect filter over that bad pic and affixing the right hashtags. I know selfie sticks weren't made for my convenience; they were created to hide my double chin. Let's be real about it. The appearance of success is an entire industry today.

But maintaining appearances isn't something we do only on social media. This is not a twenty-first-century problem; it's a human problem. For thousands of years, people have dressed up their careers with job titles that make them sound more important than they are. People use credit to purchase things to make it look like they are pulling in high-roller salaries. Sometimes we run around like mini tornadoes, rushing from one thing to another because we've convinced ourselves that the busier we look, the more important we will seem.

And the ironic thing is, you probably are fairly successful. You might even be *highly* successful. But when maintaining that appearance of success becomes your full-time job, you're in trouble. Here's why this is so dangerous: If you're not careful, you'll let the external noise of success distract you from focusing on the internal work that will lead you to growth. Moreover, the appearance of success is a moving target. It depends on who's looking at any given moment. One person's version of success might mean nothing to someone else. Consequently, you can quickly find yourself changing and adapting to suit your audience. You can be a chameleon and change constantly, but eventually you'll be somebody that nobody recognizes.

To my parents I want to appear financially independent and responsible.

To my ex who follows me on social media, I want to appear as though I have cash to burn on excessive adventures.

I want my neighbors to think I have the best house in the neighborhood.

I want my friends from college to think I'm the same old fun me, only richer.

I want my spouse to think I'm a changed person, responsible and serious about life.

And it goes on and on. We get caught up in the game of meeting everyone else's expectations of success.

But here's a question we all need to wrestle to the ground: *If the game isn't ultimately about appearing successful, am I willing to lose all that in order to win?* In other words, would you be willing to allow some of the veneer of your success to fade, to get real and honest about yourself, your faults, your fears, your weaknesses, and places where you are emotionally unhealthy in order to heal and grow as a leader?

See, here's the thing. You and I aren't going to change the system. We don't start there. Instead, we live by different values and different priorities. I firmly believe it is worth being perceived as a loser by others so that we can win the race. And your leadership is no different. Don't spend the precious years of your leadership life peacocking for others. The applause will fade. And you'll have little to show for it. Instead, spend your days becoming a leader worth following—the sort of leader whose influence doesn't wane when external pressures and distractions bombard them.

Here's a practice to help you combat this common distraction. So often, we lead for the appearance of success because we want the pat on the back, the immediate reward for the least amount of effort. So the secret to resisting this distraction is leading with the future in mind. When you're thinking ten, fifteen, and twenty years down the road, dropping the shiny exterior of success is nothing more than a short-term loss.

Great investors know this principle well. Investing in the stock market is fraught with constant uncertainty. From day to day, stocks that began with great promise can suddenly dip and soon look worthless. Good investors know when to ride it out. When the market recovers and the value begins to rise again, they know they've made the right decision. But what makes a truly great investor is not how they respond when a stock is down. No, what sets apart the truly great investors, the Warren Buffets from the Warren Bluff-its, is how they react when a stock value is up. When a stock's value is rising, some investors want to sell and make a quick profit. *It might not get better than this!* So they sell up and make a quick few bucks on their investment. But great investors know when to hold on. They're thinking future! They didn't buy these stocks on a whim. They did their homework and considered where the market is going in the future. They know there will be a few more ups and downs before they're ready to cash in. And when they hold on, they make exponentially more than those who wanted a short-term gain.

Think for a second about what it would have been like to own shares in the early days of industry-leading companies like Coca-Cola or Apple. Watching those share prices rise would have been exhilarating—intoxicating even. But imagine if you had sold up and cashed out within the first five or ten years. How frustrating would it be to watch those shares go through the roof, knowing you'd given up your future fortune for a short-term profit today? In biblical language, that's the sort of thing that leads to "weeping and gnashing of teeth."

Your leadership and personal influence are among the greatest things you'll invest in during your lifetime. Please don't throw away your long-term success for a short-term win. Don't give up the learning, growth, and development to spend your time on the distraction of appearing successful. Or as Alexander Hamilton would say, "Don't throw away your shot!"

So what happens when a leader is distracted by the appearance of success? I'm reminded of those moving sidewalks you see in airports. I love those things. When I'm in a rush and trying to catch my connecting flight while carrying two suitcases and three children and running down a long terminal building, I love to see that moving sidewalk. I know it will give me that extra little boost toward the gate before it closes and I'm stuck overnight in Cleveland. It also makes me feel like I have superpowers, but that's beside the point.

Yet while I love those moving walkways, nothing is more exasperating when I'm trying to get somewhere fast than that guy who has decided to just stand on the path with his luggage strewn around him. I want to shout, "You're missing the point!" These things are there to help you get where you want to go faster, not to move you forward at a snail's pace as you relax and check Twitter!

So what's my point in all this? Those moving sidewalks remind me of what happens to leaders who have been distracted by the appearance of success.

They stand still and relax.

They're technically moving forward and seem like they're moving toward their goals. They appear successful. But they will quickly be passed by the leaders who are still putting in the hard work of growth and development. Success can easily become a distraction that sets you up for long-term failure. Don't let your short-term wins take you out of the game.

MOVE FAST, BREAK THINGS

All this talk about moving forward is a perfect transition into the second member of our Axis of Distraction—the *allure of progress*.

We all know progress is addictive. It's hardwired into us. Even something as simple as opening an advent calendar can bring it out in me. I experience a wonderful pleasure in opening those little windows every day before Christmas, a pleasure that goes beyond the reward of that little piece of candy hidden inside. Opening the next window triggers something deep inside each of us—the allure of progress.

A friend of mine had been trying to shed some excess weight he'd put on during the first few years of his marriage. It wasn't all that much, maybe about twenty pounds, but he struggled to lose it despite trying all sorts of different diets and exercise regimens. He was becoming increasingly discouraged by how little weight he had lost, especially when he saw other people who, with the slightest effort, seemed to lose a small child's worth of weight in no time at all. Soon he found himself in a perpetual cycle. He couldn't stick with any particular program long enough for it to make a difference. He would get frustrated by his extra weight, vow to do something about it, then give up when it didn't seem to be working.

He continued in this cycle until he got an Apple Watch and tracked his diet and exercise through a few apps. Soon he was using measuring cups to portion out how much cheese he'd put in his quesadilla. He would scan the barcode on packaged food to figure out how many calories it contained. If he forgot to wear his Apple Watch, he wouldn't work out that day since his hard work wouldn't count toward his weekly exercise statistics. He became obsessed with making healthy food choices and hitting the gym every day.

Why the change?

Because what had once been nebulous and invisible had now become something concrete, measurable, and visible. He now had a way to track and monitor the work he was doing. For the first time he could see his progress—and it was addictive.

While our desire for progress can be a powerful asset and can help us make healthy lifestyle changes, it can also become another form of distraction.

I live in a city with some of the worst traffic the world has ever seen. The average Atlanta driver spends 70.8 hours stuck in traffic every year.[1] Not to mention that our reputation for dealing poorly with inclement weather conditions might well be warranted. As mentioned earlier, we experienced the "Snowpocalypse" (or "Snowmageddon") in 2014, and more recently, an enterprising soul set fire to a plastic lawn chair under an interstate overpass, and soon the entire thing was ablaze. Atlanta had 99 problems, and a bridge was one.

I say all this to point out that I hate sitting in traffic.

I know that doesn't make me unique. I'm sure you hate it too. Sitting in traffic is the worst. And what I've noticed is that I will avoid this time-waster at all costs. My disdain for being stationary manifests itself when I'm selecting my travel route. If I have a choice between a route where I'll sit in traffic for any length of time and a route that avoids traffic but takes longer overall, I'll choose the longer one simply so I can keep moving. Rather than taking the most direct route or the shortest route, I take the one that keeps me moving. I'll go all over the map just to keep the wheels spinning.

We do the same thing in our leadership. Sometimes we'll waste time spinning our wheels just to feel like we're going somewhere, when actually all we're doing is depleting our gas tanks. We don't want to wait. We like to see things passing by, some movement, to know that something—anything—is happening. So we stack our calendars with meetings. We require that every minor decision get our approval. We gamble on risky ventures to feel like we're doing something.

Do you know what that's called? It's the allure of progress. And it's a dangerous distraction. All leaders have a voice in their head telling them they must keep charging ahead, must keep the machine moving forward. If we're not moving, we're losing.

A friend of mine works with Facebook, and not long ago he told me that the company had changed one of its corporate mottos. The motto had been: "Move fast and break things." I don't know about you, but I think that motto sounds really cool. It's exactly the sort of thing you'd expect from a company willing to kill the sacred cows and move an entire industry into the future. It's extremely movement centric. And it's a motto birthed out of the allure of progress.

Facebook changed the motto when they discovered that their workforce, composed of exceptionally smart and driven people, constantly in perpetual motion, might be tempted to break the very things they needed for their success. Sometimes the emphasis on moving fast and breaking things led to people moving *too* fast. When you're told every day that you should move fast and break things, you might not take enough time to weigh the cost of your decisions. Moving fast and breaking things can keep things rolling, but it can also be destructive.

If you don't take it too far, it's a great motto. But if you let it run away with you, you'll move too fast and crash.

Progress is great. But lasting progress is something achieved over time, and it includes seasons of rest, practice, and preparation. If you want to create an excellent business strategy, you might need to spend more time strategizing rather than trying to build the airplane while you're flying and then watching parts of your life and career fall off and hurtle toward the ground. Some of the most successful people I know schedule dedicated "thinking time" into their calendars. They refuse to be distracted by the allure of progress. Stopping to think can feel like doing nothing. It can feel like a waste of time. But successful people know they need to slow down and work on what matters.

Something great leaders learn is that process can be more important than progress. Sometimes you must throw out the playbook and do things differently for the sake of progress. But there are also seasons of trusting the process, of working on the small stuff that matters to set you up for your next season of progress.

LIAR, LIAR

There's one last associate in our Axis of Distraction. Before I tell you what it is, let me ask you a question: What do you do when everyone in the room is looking to you for an answer you don't have?

Think about it. Perhaps it was the last time your boss asked for an off-the-cuff pitch on a new project. Or maybe it was the last time your direct reports asked what they should do about a problem flagged by recent data.

What do you do when you're put in that situation?

If you're anything like the rest of us, you likely go grasping for certainty, a sense that you know what you are talking about and have a solution, even if you don't. That's the final member of the Axis of Distraction: the *attraction of certainty*.

I want to look like I know what I'm talking about. Even in writing this book, I want to be sure I come across as credible. No one wants to look like an incompetent fool. We have dignity and self-respect and we want to provide answers and helpful guidance for the people we care about. I want to help my employees solve problems. I want to be a source of great ideas for my boss.

The attraction of certainty is a dangerous distraction to our leadership because it leads us to compromise our integrity. In our longing to appear confident and certain, we become liars.

It won't surprise you to learn that humans are incredibly adept at creating lies and making up stories. Ninety percent of children have grasped the concept of lying and are able to put it to good use by the age of four.[2] But it's in adulthood that we really hone the skill. A 2002 study by the University of Massachusetts found that 60 percent of adults are unable to conduct a conversation of longer than ten minutes without telling a lie.[3] And if that sounds bad, it gets even worse. Of those who lied, researchers found they told an average of three lies per conversation.[4] Sometimes we lie about things that aren't even that important, just to protect our reputation or status in a group.

We all crave certainty in uncertain times, and leaders are prone to provide that certainty whether they have good reason to do so . . . or not. I've sat in meetings with people who have pulled numbers out of the air with a finger snap to argue their point. Were their numbers accurate? Not at all. But they wanted to *appear* certain, because certainty is attractive. If you can exude confidence, people will buy what you say.

In fact, studies have shown that people will follow the person who appears most confident and certain, even if the slightest application of common sense would indicate that person has absolutely no idea what they're talking about. Although this phenomenon occurs in many areas of life, it is most common in our politics.

But here's why this brand of leadership is so poisonous. People will follow you while you wing it—*for a while*. But when your duplicity becomes known, you will lose credibility and sacrifice your integrity. People don't follow leaders they can't trust. They may go along with the program out of fear, but you will have lost trust and with that, any influence you may have had.

The alternative is simple, but it is not easy: *authenticity.*

Authentic leaders are comfortable letting others know they don't have all the answers. When you become an authentic leader, you give up the need to always be right, to always have the answer to every problem. You are okay with saying, "I don't know. Let's figure this out together." Admitting there are times when you're uncertain is a mark of humility, and this willingness to be open and honest is what gives you the opportunity to lead. Leaders who admit their uncertainty by facing it and seeking solutions will end up leading others to find answers to their problems. I'd rather be a leader who acknowledges his uncertainty and leads someone else to find the right answer than a leader who fakes it and has the wrong answer.

Being authentic, honest, and humble is not easy. It requires you to embrace vulnerability and self-awareness, qualities some of us are not comfortable showing to others. But vulnerable leaders will earn trust and increase their influence.

Maximizing your influence will mean resisting the attraction of certainty. Some problems require nuance, not certainty, and the danger is that our quest for certainty can lead us to oversimplify a complex problem. When the stakes are high, you can't afford to bludgeon a sensitive issue with your brute certainty.

Whether you see yourself as one or not, you are a leader. And your primary responsibility of leading yourself well requires you to be aware of the distractions that are most common to leadership. The distractions of the appearance of success, the allure of progress, and the appeal of certainty are some of the most difficult to fight. In the next chapter, let's look at a game plan to identify the distraction most common to you so you can learn how to filter it out.

CHAPTER 4

THE ME OF
LEADERSHIP

Whenever a weeknight event is held at our local elementary school, I try to attend. Because of my day job, I can't take off work to volunteer in the classroom or chaperone a field trip. So when "Meet the Teacher Night" comes up, I show up. And this is not me trying to brag about something I'm supposed to be doing. As Chris Rock says, "You're supposed to take care of your kids. What do you want? A cookie?" No, I'm just trying to set up this story.

When our third child, Sally, was in kindergarten, I went to meet her new teacher. As her teacher was explaining the "Dolphin Dollar" system they use at the school to reward good behavior (our mascot is the Dolphin . . . thus, Dolphin Dollars), I thought to myself, *I should probably ask Sally about that.* Our two older kids had already been through kindergarten, and I was pretty confident they had only received dollars and never would have even come close to having a dollar taken away. But with Sally, I wasn't so sure. She's more of a wild card, more like her father, who made consistent Cs in behavioral conduct for "excessive socialization."

The Dolphin Dollar system is pretty simple. You do

something good and you get a dollar; you do something you shouldn't and you lose a dollar. Collect ten dollars and on Friday, you get to choose something from the treasure box. Makes sense to me.

So that night as I was putting Sally to bed, I asked her, "Hey Sal, has your teacher ever had to take a Dolphin Dollar away?"

"Uh, yeah, she did one time," she calmly and directly responded.

"Oh . . . really?" I still have so much to learn as a parent, but one lesson I have learned is how to master my poker face whenever one of my kids tells me something even slightly negative. Don't overreact. Don't show emotion. Put on that poker face. Invite more honesty.

"So what happened?" I calmly and directly asked.

"Well, I was talking to Charlotte and the teacher asked me to stop talking, but we weren't done talking. So I kept talking and she took a dollar away from me." She told me all this in her plain and simple way, as if it had no emotional impact on her at all. At this point, I was slightly bothered but also curious.

So I pressed in for more information. "Sal, I'm a little confused. Didn't it bother you at all that you lost your dollar?"

I was surprised and confused because the treasure box is the talk of our home every Friday. It always makes its way into our family discussions, either in anticipation of buying something on Friday morning or in celebration of a prize purchased and enjoyed on Friday afternoon. So I was having a difficult time understanding how Sally could be so calm and unaffected by the loss of her dollar. That is, until she explained why . . .

"Oh no, it didn't bother me. It happened last Thursday and I knew I had eleven dollars, so I had one to give."

I was hilariously stunned, appreciative of my daughter's cleverness in working the system. Remember, you only need ten dollars to purchase something from the treasure box. I was instantly reminded of that scene from *Anchorman* when Ron Burgundy comes home and talks with his dog. "You pooped in the refrigerator? And you ate the whole wheel of cheese? How'd you do that? Heck, I'm not even mad—that's amazing!"[1]

In that moment, I also thought to myself, *Clearly, I've met my match.* I knew we would have trouble in those teenage years. But for now, I told her she needed to obey her teacher and that I love her. We prayed and I kissed her good night.

Then I found my wife so we could laugh together.

THE SUBTLE DANGER OF PROXY

We're all guilty of sacrificing the big picture, the long-term gain, for what's right in front of us. When we're too focused on results, it's easy to miss what's happening on the inside, and one of the greatest distractions any of us faces is the temptation to fixate on the external and downplay the internal. Instead of paying attention to our emotional health, we stuff it down and mask what's within, focusing on external results. As we've seen, this white noise can become an addictive "solution," keeping us from doing the work that is needed to care for our souls.

While the external distractions in our lives are varied and unique, don't think this temptation is a twenty-first-century problem. It has been around forever. Jesus warned the religious leaders of his day, the Pharisees, of the dangers of focusing too much on the outside, of counting the external signs of success, while forsaking the health of their interior lives. He put them on blast[2] by calling out their external focus and criticizing them for neglecting the things God cares about—their inner motives, desires, and beliefs—and putting on a show for the applause of people and the approval of others. The outward signs did not match the inner reality. He said to them, "Woe to you, teachers of the law and Pharisees, you hypocrites! You are like whitewashed tombs, which look beautiful on the outside but on the inside are full of the bones of the dead and everything unclean" (Matthew 23:27). Whitewash was a form of paint that was used to cover up stains or messes. Instead of cleaning the outside of the tomb, people would apply a coat of whitewash to cover up the filth.

All of us are guilty of doing this, because it's just easier. Even worse, we begin to distract ourselves with the appearance of success, the allure of progress, or the attraction of certainty. We focus on what can be easily measured, what can be seen and quantified. Yet all the while, something unhealthy is growing in the places unseen. And when we fail to pay attention to the inner life, we rob ourselves of our best opportunity to grow as leaders. We steal from our future. We cheat those we lead and ourselves.

Too often, the external becomes our proxy.

I confess. I wasn't familiar with the concept of proxies until I read Jeff Bezos's letter to his shareholders in 2016. Whether you're a fan of Amazon or not, it has undeniably become a modern giant, making Bezos one of the wealthiest leaders on the planet. In his 2017 shareholder letter, he implores his shareholders to adopt the culture he's cultivating in his company. The letter reminded me of the way football coaches will sometimes use a press conference to send a message to their team.

Bezos uses the terms *Day 1* and *Day 2* to highlight the kind of culture that has allowed Amazon to succeed and to identify the kind of culture Amazon must resist. "Day 2," he says, "is stasis. Followed by irrelevance. Followed by excruciating, painful decline. Followed by death. And *that* is why it is *always* Day 1." To maintain Day 1 culture, Amazon must pay attention to four things, and one of those is to "resist proxies." He writes:

> As companies get larger and more complex, there's a tendency to manage to proxies. This comes in many shapes and sizes, and it's dangerous, subtle, and very Day 2.
>
> A common example is process as proxy. Good process serves you so you can serve customers. But if you're not watchful, the process can become the thing. This can happen very easily in large organizations. The process becomes the proxy for the result you want. You stop looking at outcomes and just make sure you're doing the process right. Gulp. It's not that rare to hear a junior leader defend a bad outcome with something like, "Well, we followed the process." A more experienced leader will use it as an opportunity to investigate and improve the process. The process is not the thing. It's always worth asking, do we own the process or does the process own us? In a Day 2 company, you might find it's the second.[3]

When I read this letter, I immediately understood what Bezos was talking about. If I could rephrase and simplify his point, I'd say "resisting proxies" is being careful not to focus on the wrong things. No leader is immune from misplaced focus, even the head of one of the world's largest retailers. Focusing on secondary things is unavoidable at times and can even be addictive. But when we take our attention from the main thing, we get caught up managing a proxy. We constantly have to resist the temptations that keep us from paying attention to those things that need the most attention—in particular, our emotional health.

External factors will always fight to become the dominant proxy for determining success. But as a growing leader, you are only as healthy as your emotional self-awareness. Learn to resist the proxies in your life and keep your focus on what matters most.

YOU CAN'T GROW IF YOU DON'T KNOW

Here's a recap of where we've been:

- The world around us is filled with distractions that are constantly trying to draw us off track and derail our leadership.
- Most people use white noise to mask these distractions, but the benefits of masking have a hidden cost. Masking hides our emotions, often the negative ones we don't want to acknowledge, and makes us emotionally unhealthy, unaware of how we actually feel and what is truly motivating us.
- Many leaders solve this problem by turning up the noise. They increase their activities, search for new distractions, and get trapped in the Axis of Distraction—the appearance of success, the allure of progress, and the attraction of certainty.

- The answer is to turn down the noise. You cannot be emotionally oblivious and emotionally healthy at the same time. Emotional health begins with becoming emotionally aware, and this requires listening to what's happening on the inside.

In this chapter, I want to help you avoid the distractions of the world and instead train yourself to turn down the noise and listen. Be forewarned, however. The practices I am suggesting and the habits you must develop will make you uncomfortable. They may hurt. But over time, they will help you become more emotionally aware.

I can promise you this: you'll never be the leader you want to be if you don't learn these things. Without self-awareness—an understanding of who you are, what you feel, and why you do the things you do—you will not be emotionally healthy. And the last thing the world needs is more leaders who are emotionally constipated, sick with an inner disease they don't even realize they have.

Becoming emotionally aware requires you to learn how to study yourself. You need to understand what's happening inside you, and as you grow in self-awareness, you become more emotionally intelligent. You've likely worked with difficult people who are unaware of how their emotions and behaviors are affecting others. And nothing is worse than having to make an unaware person aware of something everyone but that person knows. It's one of the most difficult tasks in leadership. I'm not sure who invented the phrase "What you don't know can't hurt you," but it's one of the dumbest sayings in the English language.

What you don't know *can* hurt you. It can destroy your life and take you out as a leader. The number one reason leaders crash and burn is that they're unaware of something about themselves—or at the very least are unwilling to face it and admit it. Those things you don't know about yourself have already hurt you, they will hurt you, and they are probably hurting you right now as you read this. The same is true for me. What I don't know about myself is hurting me even as I write this.

Awareness is as powerful as unawareness is problematic. That's why the old cliché is still true: the secret of leadership is knowing yourself. You can't get where you want to go if you don't know where you are. But even more basic than knowing where you are is knowing who you are. And a leader who doesn't know themself is a dangerous guide.

That's why self-awareness is sometimes referred to as emotional intelligence. As you grow more intelligent about your own emotions, you will be better able to help others understand their own emotions. But it all begins with you.

Too often we allow our emotions to sit in the driver's seat, taking up that leadership space without any interrogation or confrontation. Whether consciously or unconsciously, we let our emotions run our lives. Many effective leaders are able to manage and adapt, covering their feelings and hiding their desires and drives in acceptable ways. But unless they're dealt with directly, our emotions will eventually control our lives.

Just think about the last "emotional" purchase you made. You were surfing on Amazon, with nothing in particular in mind. Or maybe you were scrolling through Facebook and an ad appeared for an item strangely similar to that thing you

A leader who doesn't know themself is a dangerous guide.

searched for three hours ago (funny how that happens). *Act now! Last one available! These are going fast!* Marketers use these high-pressure phrases to play on our fear of missing out, leading us to buy something we don't want and probably won't even use. What's driving all this? Our emotions—those desires and drives within us that we may or may not be fully aware of but are currently occupying the driver's seat. Unless you and I are ruthlessly curious about our emotions, they'll end up controlling us.

Learning to manage your emotions is a skill like any other skill in life. Spend time working on it and you get better at it. Hone the skill and it will become easier for you. But allow it to sit on the shelf for an extended period of time and you'll find that, unlike riding a bike, you can't just pick it right back up. Become an emotional detective to become more emotionally aware, because if you don't know, you can't grow.

BECOMING AN EMOTIONAL DETECTIVE

As a parent, I've discovered that one of my greatest challenges is appropriately and effectively monitoring the use of technology in our home. The struggle is real. As adults, we know the addictive power our devices have over our lives. We can make efforts to resist and guard ourselves. But children cannot. In one of his opening monologues, Jimmy Fallon joked, "Studies have shown that it costs $600,000 to raise a kid. Or for $600 you can just buy an iPad." Ah, very true, Jimmy.

There are many unanswered questions about our use (and abuse) of technology. How early is too early for a baby to sit before a screen? How much screen time is too much screen time for elementary-aged children? Does it count as screen time if they're doing their homework on a screen? If you have kids yourself, you know how challenging these questions can be.

My wife, Jenny, and I started using technology early with our kids. I'm not proud of that, and I don't advise it to others, but to use one of the most worthless phrases ever, "It is what it is." Oh, and you can judge all you want, but unless you're raising Albert Einstein's great-great-grandkids, the chances of your child becoming another young Einstein are slim to quite slim. Sometimes handing the kid a screen is the easiest way to fix the problem.

Yes, I realize we chose to have five kids, and so life tends to get a little chaotic at times. Sometimes just being able to get the grocery shopping done with a crying one-year-old requires a screen. Or when that one-year-old has been screaming for the last hour and we're still sitting in traffic, trying to get home from the zoo, why would we not turn on some sort of video to calm the crying? And at the end of the day, when I've lost all ability to speak kindly, maintain any amount of patience, and answer any more questions about Elmo's eating habits, why wouldn't I use a thirty-minute show as motivation to get through dinner and bath time? Honestly!

There are loads of problems we don't have time to wade through, but if I'm honest, our use of technology is one that constantly bothers me. I'm bothered by the unknown of what our kids are learning—and not learning—because we're shoving screens in their faces at such young ages. I'm concerned that we're jeopardizing their creative abilities to play without a screen. When I was a kid, boredom forced us to create games, and we played the dumbest games we could invent because we had to. I played the ever-popular basketball shoot-out in my bedroom with a trash can and a balled-up piece of paper because that was about all there was to do. I once heard someone say it takes at least fifteen minutes of boredom before kids begin to exercise their creativity. If that's true, we may be stealing the imagination of an entire generation by giving them mindless distractions just to keep them from being bored.

But this isn't true only of our children. We've all had that bizarre experience of sitting in the waiting room of a doctor's office and looking up from our smartphones to realize every other person is staring at a screen. Worse, we've all sat in a room with five people we know, waiting for a meeting to start, yet still choosing to stare at our devices instead of talking to one another. If it takes fifteen minutes of boredom for our creativity to kick in, then how much silence, solitude, and boredom must we suffer before we are able to actually hear what is going on inside us? The masking effects of white noise are stronger than we realize, and it takes intentionality to actively turn down the noise in our lives. Great leaders turn down the noise low enough and long enough to be ruthlessly curious about their emotions.

One of the skills we must learn to cultivate is emotional curiosity. Justin, one of my coworkers, remarked to me the other day, "Noise and distraction kill our curiosity." How true that is! Emotionally healthy leaders are those who have learned, often through trial and error, to eliminate the distractions in their lives and turn down the noise because they are *curious*. They are emotional detectives, ready to listen, evaluate, and discover new things about themselves. And this work will take time. You will need to choose to make it a habit.

Chances are you can't become an emotional detective on your own. You're probably going to need someone you trust to help you process your discoveries. The goal is to make emotional work a habit in your life, something you practice on a daily basis. To help you cultivate emotional curiosity, I want to give you a simple formula to remember. Emotional detective work requires three simple steps: identify the emotion, find language for the emotion, and then deal directly with the emotion.

Noise and distraction kill our curiosity.

Listen to Your Emotions

Have you ever cried in front of your boss? A few months ago, I did. I'm about to turn forty years old, and other than being moved by an inspirational movie, I've never cried in a meeting. I'm not saying I'm against crying in meetings, but I'm certainly not for it. If you had opened up and shared with me that you had cried in a meeting in front of your boss, I wouldn't have overtly made fun of you for doing it, but I would've judged you a little bit for failing to manage your emotions in a professional setting. Of course, that was before my own little emotional explosion.

The church I lead is one of seven churches in the Atlanta area, all under the umbrella of our larger organization. Nearly every Tuesday, we have a two-hour meeting with the lead pastors of our campuses, plus our management team. We focus on planning, problem solving, and collaboration. These are my direct peers and all the people who are above me in the organization—my bosses. They're all in this meeting.

Most of the time, it's an upbeat, inspiring time filled with new ideas and excitement about the future. But this particular Tuesday was different. A set of dashboards—visual status updates on the state of each of our churches—was passed around the room, and the one for my particular church looked quite gloomy. But worse than getting a bad report, I felt like the data misrepresented things that were not under my direct control and the conclusions were unfair. I held my emotions in check during the meeting, but I couldn't shake how I was feeling. Even worse, I couldn't exactly determine *what* I was feeling.

The moment passed, and I left the meeting and went on to the next thing. A few days later, I had my finger on the white noise knob of my life and was turning up the activity, keeping things busy, making sure my schedule was full. For some reason, I decided to take a break, and I slipped out for a fifteen-minute walk to one of our adjacent office buildings. I soon realized that the emotions from that earlier meeting still deeply affected me. I mistakenly diagnosed my emotion as anger, assuming I was mad at my boss for the way he had handled the meeting. Because we have a good relationship, I thought to myself, *I should just sit down with him this afternoon to clear the air.* And so we did.

As we talked, I realized my main emotion wasn't anger. It was deeper, and it was worse. The longer we talked, the more confused I became, and after about twenty minutes of back-and-forth miscommunication, I felt myself starting to lose it. The more I talked, the worse it became, and suddenly the awkwardness, the embarrassment, and several actual alligator-sized tears arrived at about the same time. In my life, those three amigos seem to travel together. At that point, there was no more masking, no more white noise to cover up my feelings. We sat together in that awkward silence as I allowed myself to listen to what was happening inside me.

As a pastor, I've been in loads of meetings with hurting people trying to communicate through tears. It puts the listener in a bit of an awkward spot. Do I hand him a tissue? Do I sit silently and give her time to pull it together? Do I offer some words of encouragement to try to help? I could tell that my boss was feeling all that. Realizing that I was dealing with something heavier than a misrepresented dashboard, my boss kindly asked if he could pray for me. I said to him, "You're welcome to pray for me, but please do it later. I think I need to leave." I walked out, got in my car, and lost it.

For an hour, I sobbed and sobbed and sobbed. Where was all this coming from? I could feel the strength of the emotion, but I had no idea what was driving it, what lay behind it all. Somewhere on my drive home, the clouds parted and I was able to identify and name what I was feeling. It became as clear as finding Waldo on the page. Once you see him, you can't *unsee* him—it's obvious he's there. Not only was I able to identify the emotion, but I also found the words to describe what it was and why I was feeling it. (We'll get to that in just a bit.)

Being able to accurately identify that emotion was glorious! Seriously, it felt like taking ibuprofen for a bad headache. Identifying the emotion didn't change the emotion or lessen the strength of the emotion, but it did give me hope. And that's the first thing I want you to know. Until you can identify the emotions inside you, they will stay right there, locked up inside you. If you fail to listen to them, they will simply sit there, hidden and unexpressed. And as I had just found out in an extremely awkward way, those hidden emotions can wreak havoc until they are named and dealt with.

Here's the thing. As long as you keep your fingers on that volume knob, regulating the white noise of your busy schedule and masking your feelings with the appearance of success or another habit of distraction, those emotions will continue to accumulate and build. They will fill the cracks and crevices of your heart, waiting to be identified and longing to be felt. In a sudden and surprising way, I learned I had been suppressing emotions that were trying to tell me something deeply important about myself, but I hadn't made the time to listen to them, name them, or reflect on what they were trying to communicate. And, unfortunately, the dam of my emotions broke. The white noise machine suddenly stopped working.

In the silence that remained, I was able to hear those emotions I'd been suppressing, and I was able to identify exactly what I was feeling.

If you are a leader, you can't afford to lose it. In this case, my boss understood and my mini meltdown didn't shipwreck my life or my leadership. But why take the risk? Each of us faces a choice. You can choose to turn down the noise on your own or, like my embarrassing episode, you can wait until the noise machine breaks and the noise is turned down for you.

My hope is that you will accept the challenge to cultivate emotional curiosity. Until you identify what you're feeling, you can't learn to manage it, and if you don't manage your emotions, they will eventually manage you.

Name Your Emotions

Learning to become an emotional detective is like learning a foreign language. The more you speak, the more familiar and comfortable you become with words and phrases. You may even begin to develop an accent! As you learn to speak in emotional language, you will start out by simply naming what you are feeling. You'll develop a vocabulary to describe how you feel. And as your vocabulary grows, you'll become better at identifying and naming your emotions.

Unfortunately, the opposite is true as well.

I have several friends who studied Spanish in high school. If you never grow beyond your high school Spanish 101 class, you'll be stuck with a limited vocabulary and a few primitive phrases. You know these won't suffice if you want to communicate with a native Spanish speaker. Comedian Brian Regan talks about the difference between the Spanish he learned in Spanish class and the Spanish he would hear on South Beach in Miami. Mimicking an older Cuban man smoking a fat cigar, he says, *"There are many books in the library . . . The tractor is red . . . I have a canary and it is pretty."*[4]

You may learn phrases like these in the classroom, and knowing them will help you pass the class, but they won't help you if you are dropped alone in the middle of Mexico. And they won't help you establish a relationship with someone. To progress beyond basic communication skills, your vocabulary needs to grow. You will need to learn the language to the point where you start to think in that language. And the longer you speak the language, the easier it becomes. Words are translated in your thoughts, and the new language becomes second nature.

The same is true as we learn the language of feelings. And like a foreign language, it won't come naturally at first. It is going to require some work.

Over the past few years, I've been trying to grow my emotional vocabulary. To help me, I've kept something called a "feelings chart" on my desk (see p. 98). As I tried to identify my feelings on a more regular basis, I found myself limited by the feeling words I knew. My vocabulary limited my ability to articulate and name what I was feeling. Having the chart near me has been extremely helpful in expanding my vocabulary.

Don't be ashamed if you find yourself needing something like this. Many of us weren't taught the language of feelings in our families. Maybe we've never had people in our lives who talked about their feelings or asked us to talk about ours. I had a buddy who had recently been through an addiction recovery program and was making some changes in his life. Without the white noise of his addiction masking his feelings any longer, he was realizing he had all sorts of pent-up emotional energy inside him that was looking for a way out. Years of stuffing and avoiding his emotions had limited his emotional competence. He knew he was emotionally immature, and his road to recovery required him to enroll in a foreign language class—learning a new vocabulary to release those emotions by listening to them and naming them. Over time, he was able to grow in emotional awareness by communicating what he was feeling with greater accuracy and regularity. He even wore a large wristband with a list of emotions attached to help him quickly name what he was feeling. I realize it sounds bizarre, walking around the office like Peyton Manning with a cheat sheet on your wristband. But he knew firsthand the alternative. Years of failing to name his emotions clearly had not worked and, in fact, had led to several painful and embarrassing outcomes.

As I drove home after my embarrassing meeting with my boss, I approached my heart like Inspector Clouseau rummaging through a crime scene. I found I was frantically looking for the language to name what I was feeling. The metrics on the dashboard were saying I was a failure. And I felt like a failure, which meant I was experiencing these emotions:

Shame.

Inadequacy.

Discouragement.

As I drove alone in my car, I named those emotions out loud. Naming them was like hitting the play button. With each naming, I was inviting that feeling to speak to me.

And as the words came out of my mouth, the volume and intensity of my sobs grew stronger. It was as if naming them gave them permission to talk louder. But as much as it hurt to name them, I also knew it was badly needed. Words are keys to unlock the vault where emotions are hidden. Until we name them, our feelings are incarcerated, behind bars, unable to communicate with us in healthy ways. Why had I—either intentionally or unintentionally—locked up those feelings? I wasn't sure, but I knew I didn't like what these emotions were trying to tell me about myself. I wasn't yet ready to admit that I felt like a failure because saying it out loud made me feel weak, and I didn't like that.

Even after we have *identified* the emotion and *named* the emotion, we still have much work to do. In fact, this is where the long-term work begins. We start to deal with the emotion by asking it questions.

	Happiness	Caring	Depression	Inadequateness	Fear
STRONG	Delighted Ebullient Ecstatic Elated Energetic Enthusiastic Euphoric Excited Exhilarated Overjoyed Thrilled Tickled pink Turned on Vibrant Zippy	Adoring Ardent Cherishing Compassionate Crazy about Devoted Doting Fervent Idolizing Infatuated Passionate Wild about Worshipful Zealous	Alienated Barren Beaten Bleak Bleeding Dejected Depressed Desolate Despondent Dismal Empty Gloomy Grieved Grim Hopeless In despair Woeful Worried	Blemished Blotched Broken Crippled Damaged False Feeble Finished Flawed Helpless Impotent Inferior Invalid Powerless Useless Washed up Whipped Worthless Zero	Alarmed Appalled Desperate Distressed Frightened Horrified Intimidated Panicky Paralyzed Petrified Shocked Terrified Terror-stricken Wrecked
MEDIUM	Aglow Buoyant Cheerful Elevated Gleeful Happy In high spirits Jovial Light-hearted Lively Merry Riding high Sparkling Up	Admiring Affectionate Attached Fond Fond of Huggy Kind Kind-hearted Loving Partial Soft on Sympathetic Tender Trusting Warm-hearted	Awful Blue Crestfallen Demoralized Devalued Discouraged Dispirited Distressed Downcast Downhearted Fed up Lost Melancholy Miserable Regretful Rotten Sorrowful Tearful Upset Weepy	Ailing Defeated Deficient Dopey Feeble Helpless Impaired Imperfect Incapable Incompetent Incomplete Ineffective Inept Insignificant Lacking Lame Overwhelmed Small Substandard Unimportant	Afraid Apprehensive Awkward Defensive Fearful Fidgety Fretful Jumpy Nervous Scared Shaky Skittish Spineless Taut Threatened Troubled Wired
LIGHT	Contented Cool Fine Genial Glad Gratified Keen Pleasant Pleased Satisfied Serene Sunny	Appreciative Attentive Considerate Friendly Interested in Kind Like Respecting Thoughtful Tolerant Warm toward Yielding	Blah Disappointed Down Funk Glum Low Moody Morose Somber Subdued Uncomfortable Unhappy	Dry Incomplete Meager Puny Tenuous Tiny Uncertain Unconvincing Unsure Weak Wishful	Anxious Careful Cautious Disquieted Goose-bumpy Shy Tense Timid Uneasy Unsure Watchful Worried

Confusion	Hurt	Anger	Loneliness	Remorse
Baffled	Abused	Affronted	Abandoned	Abashed
Befuddled	Aching	Belligerent	Black	Debased
Chaotic	Anguished	Bitter	Cut off	Degraded
Confounded	Crushed	Burned up	Deserted	Delinquent
Confused	Degraded	Enraged	Destroyed	Depraved
Dizzy	Destroyed	Fuming	Empty	Disgraced
Flustered	Devastated	Furious	Forsaken	Evil
Rattled	Discarded	Heated	Isolated	Exposed
Reeling	Disgraced	Incensed	Marooned	Humiliated
Shocked	Forsaken	Infuriated	Neglected	Judged
Shook up	Humiliated	Intense	Ostracized	Mortified
Speechless	Mocked	Outraged	Outcast	Shamed
Startled	Punished	Provoked	Rejected	Sinful
Stumped	Rejected	Seething	Shunned	Wicked
Stunned	Ridiculed	Storming		Wrong
Taken-aback	Ruined	Truculent		
Thrown	Scorned	Vengeful		
Thunderstruck	Stabbed	Vindictive		
Trapped	Tortured	Wild		
Adrift	Annoyed	Aggravated	Alienated	Apologetic
Ambivalent	Belittled	Annoyed	Alone	Ashamed
Bewildered	Cheapened	Antagonistic	Apart	Contrite
Puzzled	Criticized	Crabby	Cheerless	Culpable
Blurred	Damaged	Cranky	Companionless	Demeaned
Disconcerted	Depreciated	Exasperated	Dejected	Downhearted
Disordered	Devalued	Fuming	Despondent	Flustered
Disorganized	Discredited	Grouchy	Estranged	Guilty
Disquieted	Distressed	Hostile	Excluded	Penitent
Disturbed	Impaired	Ill-tempered	Left out	Regretful
Foggy	Injured	Indignant	Leftover	Remorseful
Frustrated	Maligned	Irate	Lonely	Repentant
Misled	Marred	Irritated	Oppressed	Shamefaced
Mistaken	Miffed	Offended	Uncherished	Sorrowful
Misunderstood	Mistreated	Ratty		Sorry
Mixed up	Resentful	Resentful		
Perplexed	Troubled	Sore		
Troubled	Used	Spiteful		
	Wounded	Testy		
		Ticked off		
Distracted	Let down	Bugged	Blue	Bashful
Uncertain	Minimized	Chagrined	Detached	Blushing
Uncomfortable	Neglected	Dismayed	Discouraged	Chagrined
Undecided	Put away	Galled	Distant	Chastened
Unsettled	Put down	Grim	Insulated	Crestfallen
Unsure	Rueful	Impatient	Melancholy	Embarrassed
	Tender	Irked	Remote	Hesitant
	Touched	Petulant	Separate	Humble
	Unhappy	Resentful	Withdrawn	Meek
		Sullen		Regretful
		Uptight		Reluctant
				Sheepish

Question Your Emotions

The first step to learning about something is asking questions. People who never ask questions never learn.

This is true of our emotions as well. So I had a little Q&A with myself.

I'm feeling shame, but should I be ashamed?

I had to think about that. Don't rush to quick answers here. Let yourself think about the question. Was I guilty of leading poorly? Or to say it more positively, was I guilty of not leading well enough to create growth? Maybe. But should I feel shame about that? Absolutely not.

In dealing with this emotion, I've been blessed by the insights of Dr. Brené Brown. In a very respectful way and because I like to pretend that we're besties, I call her Brenéneh as an ode to Sheneneh Jenkins from the early 1990s show *Martin* ("Oh my goodness!"). In her incredibly popular TED Talk "Listening to Shame" (the one that's been viewed several million times), Dr. Brown says, "Shame is a focus on self, guilt is a focus on behavior. Shame is, 'I am bad.' Guilt is, 'I did something bad.' How many of you, if you did something that was hurtful to me, would be willing to say, 'I'm sorry. I made a mistake'? How many of you would be willing to say that? Guilt: I'm sorry. I made a mistake. Shame: I'm sorry. I am a mistake."[5]

Dr. Brown's words rang through my head that day as I questioned my emotions. I wanted to know why I felt shame and what I needed to do with that emotion. You see, every emotion you feel is a valid emotion, one that must be listened to, named (acknowledged), and questioned. But every emotion you feel does not have the right to be in charge. We have the capacity to listen to, name, and question our emotions, and we also have the ability to disagree with them. In fact, this is a mark of emotional maturity: as you learn to understand your emotions, you can begin to take control of them. You get to determine whether you will allow an emotion to affect you and if so, *how* you will allow that emotion to affect you. Just because you feel it doesn't mean you need to internalize it.

This is where my faith intersects with the way I relate to my emotions. While I listen to them, name them, and question them, ultimately I have to discipline myself to see my emotions through the lens of how God sees me and what he has said about me. Because while understanding our emotions can lead to self-awareness, our emotions are not always right. They are products of our circumstances and of the way we interpret the things that happen to us, the choices we make, and the actions we take. But you and I are not infallible. We are often wrong. We make mistakes. We don't always understand the big picture. So we need guides to help us in separating what is right from wrong, true from false.

That's where I rely on God to guide me. If you question an emotion and what it says conflicts with what he says about you, you need to get underneath it before you let it burrow deeper inside you. Shame is particularly fickle, eager to speak into our pain and inadequacy, but whether you feel like a failure or a success, you cannot let those words define you. You must learn to confront your emotions with the truth, speaking to yourself for the sake of your own confidence and self-worth.

What about inadequacy? Should I allow myself to feel that?

This emotion was more complicated. I thought to myself, *Will there be things in my life that I can't do?* Yes, for sure. Like when I tell people I played high school baseball. I say I played, but mostly, I was a member of our school's team. The playing part didn't happen so much. Were I to place all my emotional health on whether I had succeeded in that particular area of my life, I'd definitely feel inadequate, like a terrible failure. And truth be told, my baseball skills, my desire to play, and my work ethic to train were all inadequate to play at or beyond the high school level. But my truthful inadequacy in this area of my life doesn't mean I'm inadequate as a human being. The same is true for my skills and abilities in other areas of life. Of course I'm going to run into problems I'm unable to solve. We all have areas where we are more skilled than others, but allowing my success or failure in a particular area—and the emotions that result from it—to define or label me is a recipe for disaster. Labels say more about your past than they do about your future.

Labels say more about your past than they do about your future.

Okay. What about the discouragement I'm feeling? Is that good or bad?

For the last few years, I've been meeting with a personal coach who has helped me tremendously. Roger Federer has a coach, so why shouldn't I? I have a list of learnings from him, but the one that really helped me on that crucial car ride was something he had said to me about engaging with my negative emotions: *Don't take the bait.*

In other words, don't believe what your emotions say to you. Test and evaluate. In pivotal seasons of instability, in any area of your life, there will be a recurring temptation to take the bait when you feel strong negative emotions. Whether it's the loss of a job, marital conflict, a rebellious season for a child, a financial collapse, or a bleak health prognosis, you're going to be drawn to strong feelings of insecurity and self-pity, or perhaps anger, bitterness, and resentment. It happens to all of us, and discouragement is an emotion you must deal with directly. Ask the questions. Learn what you're supposed to learn, but don't let what it says about you define you. Treat the situation as an experiment in the laboratory of life, something to be learned from, but refuse to take the bait on the negative emotions resulting from it.

"NOW OR NEVER" IS RARELY RIGHT

I didn't have to process every emotion I was feeling that day. I could have waited, but I'm glad I didn't. You'll often hear people say the words "now or never," but the truth is that it's rarely now or never. If you've started listening to your emotions but haven't gone further, haven't named or questioned them, you can start today. You can start next week. Or maybe you've already started doing some of the hard work, but you're thinking about quitting because it's getting tough. It's okay to take a break. Give yourself some space. Put it down for a bit, but don't fail to pick it back up. While it's seldom "now or never," the longer you wait, the harder it will be.

What if I had allowed the emotions I had locked inside that day to continue to fester? Most likely, they would have caused me more trouble than a few tears in front of my boss. In the long run, they might have affected my ability to lead in every area of my life. If I hadn't taken the time to deal with them, they could have shattered my confidence or smuggled bitterness into my future. Fortunately, I was afforded the space and the appropriate counselors to help me process how I was feeling.

And here's the thing. Even though I'm writing this book, I'm writing as a fellow learner on this journey. It's not over. Even as I write this, there is a temptation to call up those old voices and let them play their mind games. Or worse, there is the temptation to pull out the old white noise machine and crank up the volume again so I can mask what I'm feeling.

Neither option is healthy. Again, we must turn down the noise low enough and long enough to be ruthlessly curious, learning how to listen to our emotions, name them, and then question them. If I had never learned how to do this, I'd be nowhere near as far along on the journey toward emotional health and maturity. And by the grace of God, though I'm not near where I need to be, I'm not where I once was. It all begins with becoming an emotional detective.

In the next chapter, we'll learn another essential skill for becoming emotionally healthy. I want to teach you how to form noise-canceling habits that will allow space for this ruthless curiosity. You don't have to believe everything you think and you don't have to accept everything you feel, but until you form habits to explore those areas of your internal world, you'll always be reacting to your emotions.

But let's not move too quickly. We'll get there next. Until then, here's a quick review of where we've been in this chapter.

CHAPTER SUMMARY

1. All leaders face the strong temptation to become focused on external results while missing the internal work that emotional health requires.
2. Emotional health begins with emotional awareness. To be more aware of what's inside, you must train yourself to be an emotional detective.
3. Becoming an emotional detective requires three things: listening to your emotions, naming them, and questioning them.
4. Great leaders learn how to turn down the noise low enough and long enough to be ruthlessly curious about their emotions.
5. Internal and invisible decisions to develop emotional health will determine your leadership lid. Those invisible decisions are what will develop visible results in leadership.

CHAPTER 5

NOISE-CANCELING
HABITS

My goal in writing this book is not to try to make you more emotional. I'm not out to change your personality or turn you into a more touchy-feely person. You are already an emotional being and don't need to become *more* emotional; rather, you need to become more emotionally *aware*. You need to find space to tune in to the emotions that are already inside you. They're always saying something, trying to communicate with you. And if you don't turn down the noise low enough and long enough to pay attention, you won't be able to manage the emotion. Unless you listen to, name, and ask questions of your emotions, they will eventually manage you.

Like anything in life that really matters, emotional awareness cannot be a onetime thing. It's more than a good cry-fest or a visit to see a counselor. I'm talking about making this a habit, something that becomes routine, like brushing your teeth.

OLD HABITS DIE HARD

Our eight-year-old son is a hustler. He has always been that way. I'll never forget taking him to the park after he had just turned one. He was learning to walk and loved the newfound freedom of being able to get from point A to point B on his own. After sliding down one of the slides at our local playground, he turned around, saw where he had come from, and did what every other kid has done at one time. He tried walking up the slide. Why is walking up the slide even more fun than sliding down the slide? I watched him that afternoon as he worked tirelessly to get up that slide. Unless he was intentional and careful in putting his foot down, his tennis shoes weren't providing him with enough grip to gain the leverage he needed to scale the steep grade. But he wasn't going to stop. He was sweating profusely and hyper-focused on getting up the slide, and I had to admire his perseverance and commitment. I thought to myself, *That kid is a hustler, a real go-getter. I hope he never loses that quality.*

I thought that because I knew he would *need* that quality. He wasn't born with the superior athletic gene that makes so many athletes great. If I had that gene, I would have given it to him, but you know what they say: you can't give what you don't have. He's a decent athlete, but I know he is going to have to work hard to be better than average.

His current athletic obsession is basketball. He loves it. As soon as I'm home from work, he's waiting for me in the driveway to play one-on-one. I'm no basketball expert, so I try not to overcoach him. I simply want him to enjoy the game as much as I did as a kid. The more we've played together, the more I've noticed that he's shooting his layups incorrectly. When he's driving to the goal to shoot a layup, he jumps off his right foot on a right-handed layup, instead of jumping off the left foot. So, of course, I tried to explain why players jump off the left foot on right-handed layups and why they jump off the right foot when shooting left-handed layups. But quite honestly, I don't know the reason why, so I couldn't explain it very well. It was one of those moments in life when, as a parent, you shrug and say, "I don't know why. That's just the way it works."

Unfortunately, he kept doing it. For months I tried other ways of explaining it, but my words never made sense to him—until his basketball coach told him to fix his technique. Amazing how another adult can say the exact same thing you've been saying in slightly different words and suddenly it makes all the sense in the world. For whatever reason, as soon as his coach said something to him, it became incredibly important. He was determined to change his method.

Sadly, it hasn't been an easy fix. For all his life, every time he's jumped over a line in the street, a crack in the sidewalk, or a log in the woods, he's jumped off his right foot. So changing to the other foot is taking work. But he's not giving up. Eventually, he's going to figure it out.

My son's quest to learn to jump from a different foot is no different than our quest to change an ingrained habit in our lives. When we've spent years of our lives developing a habit, changing that habit takes work. And that's true of our emotional habits as well. If the emotions inside you have created habitual patterns, changing those habits won't happen overnight. It's going to take commitment, intentionality, and diligence to change a pattern that has become routine. Old habits die hard.

NOISE CANCELLATION

The only way to combat the old habits of distraction is to develop new habits to create space for emotional curiosity.

The only way to combat the old habits of distraction is to develop new habits to create space for emotional curiosity.

These new habits provide the framework for the next four chapters—finding the why, speaking to yourself, getting quiet, and pressing pause. Great leaders practice these habits intentionally and consistently to create and maintain emotional health. The trend line of your career progression will parallel the trend line of your emotional health. As you grow in emotional health, you will grow in influence. As you grow in influence, you will grow in opportunities. This correlation could not be more important.

Have you ever used a pair of noise-canceling headphones? They are absolutely brilliant. There are actually two different types of noise-canceling headphones—active and passive. The less interesting passive ones are typically heavier because they contain the types of materials needed to block out noise. Think of passive noise-canceling headphones as a wall built with thicker material and filled with more high-density foam and other noise-filtering materials to decrease unwanted noise. In my book, though, they don't hold a candle to active noise-canceling headphones.

The active ones are not only more effective but also way more interesting. These feats of audio magic go looking for frequencies to block out. Once they find an unwanted frequency, they create "their own sound waves that mimic the incoming noise in every respect except one: the headphone's sound waves are 180 degrees out of phase with the intruding waves. That means about 70 percent of ambient noise is effectively blocked, making noise-canceling headphones ideal for airline and train travel, open office environments, or any other location with a high level of background noise."[1] What a fantastic concept!

In the same way, for you to achieve the optimal space for

personal exploration and growth, you need to employ certain habits to cancel out the distractions interfering with your emotional health. For you to grow as a leader, or as a parent, friend, teacher, or counselor, you need to employ these habits on a daily basis. Oh, and the best part is that these habits don't cost nearly as much as noise-canceling headphones do. Interestingly, using them is free, but choosing not to use them is costly.

A CITY WITHOUT WALLS

Ever since my teenage years, I've been reading the book of wise sayings written mostly by King Solomon known as Proverbs. If you're in a new leadership role or feel like you are in over your head right now, the book of Proverbs is a great place to ground yourself in common but crucial wisdom for all areas of life. Solomon uses a wonderful word picture to show what it looks like to lack emotional awareness and health in Proverbs 25:28 (NASB): "Like a city that is broken into *and* without walls is a man who has no control over his spirit."

Envision an ancient city without the protection or sophisticated technology of our modern military. What kept people safe in ancient times? What provided citizens with a sense of safety? It was the wall that surrounded the city. Without the wall, the city was always vulnerable to attack from enemies. And in this proverb, we have a word picture describing "a man who has no control over his spirit"—an emotionally unstable person. This is someone who is easily manipulated and controlled by how they feel. Think about the person who is easily angered, the person who can't resist that impulse purchase, or that person who is easily manipulated emotionally or even sexually in a dating relationship. Like a city without walls, these people are left defenseless, easy prey for others who wish to control or take advantage of them. And all because they've failed to manage their emotions.

There are plenty of examples of this in the world of leadership as well. You don't have to look very far. It's the manager who feels threatened by a talented new hire. It's the team leader who talks too much because of his incessant need for attention. It's the analyst whose deep insecurity keeps her from speaking up out of fear of being wrong. In each example, you can probably envision some of the consequences of that person's failure to pay attention to what's happening on the inside.

THE INVISIBLE AND INTANGIBLE FORCES

Great leaders have unusual habits that create unusual behaviors. But these habits require self-leadership. You need to be intentional about moving counter to the ingrained, unhealthy habits you've formed. In some cases, you have to choose to do the opposite of what your intuition and instincts are telling you to do. For leaders who are used to "trusting their gut," that can be a difficult lesson.

George Costanza had to learn this the hard way. In one of the greatest *Seinfeld* episodes ever aired, "The Opposite," George realizes that every decision he has ever made has been wrong, and his life has become the exact opposite of what it should be. "It became very clear to me sitting out there today that every decision I've ever made, in my entire life, has been wrong. My life is the opposite of everything I want it to be.

Every instinct I have, in every aspect of life, be it something to wear, something to eat . . , It's all been wrong."[2]

The only way for George to see the results he wants to see is to intentionally do something radical—to choose the opposite of every impulse he would ever have going forward. It's a hilarious idea, but sometimes George's response is quite appropriate.

As a leader, I've found that the forces that keep me focused on external results are extremely powerful. Earlier we talked about the Axis of Distraction and the appearance of success, the allure of progress, and the attraction of certainty. Whatever you identify as a primary distraction in your life, whether it's one of the Axis members or a smaller ally like social media or online shopping, consistently turning down the white noise in your life is going to require a radical shift in you and in the choices you make. You will need to learn new, noise-canceling habits. You will have to get rid of the internal distractions so you can focus on the external actions because great leaders make invisible decisions that lead to visible results.

As you get started on the road to emotional health and greater self-awareness, everything in you is going to want to focus on the visible results. You may be drawn to the things that others praise you for, the things that earn attaboys and congratulations for a job well done. But it's the invisible habits

But it's the invisible habits of self-reflection, self-inspection, and self-discovery that will allow you to develop into the leader you want to be.

of self-reflection, self-inspection, and self-discovery that will allow you to develop into the leader you want to be.

I've seen my boss and mentor, Andy Stanley, carry out these habits with such regularity that I didn't even notice he was doing it at first. But the longer I've worked for him, the more I've come to value the personal habits of growth and development behind his leadership and effectiveness. The constant temptation for leaders is to gain power, prestige, and popularity, and then stop growing. Having arrived at the goal, they are no longer curious. They stop asking questions, sometimes to avoid the risk of having to change something or admit weakness. Every leader faces this temptation.

And that's why I value what I've learned from working with Andy. He has that position of power, prestige, and popularity in our broader organizational culture. He has what so many are searching for, yet he is still willing to look inward for the sake of self-discovery and self-evaluation. He is still, after all he has done and achieved, emotionally curious.

A few years ago, we had an extremely talented staff member leave to work at another church. Because loyalty is a highly elevated value in many churches, when a contributing member leaves, it is all too common for their departure to be seen as disloyal, even a betrayal of the mission. "Good riddance. Don't let the door hit you on the way out," describes the feeling some have when they leave. But that's not how we do things. As an organization, we choose to celebrate people when they leave, or at the very least we try to fight against the hurt feelings that are all too natural in these situations.

About three months after this staff member left our church, he had a change of heart—a complete reversal. He came back to his manager with his tail tucked between his legs, asking if he could have his old job back. We had begun the process of hiring this person back when Andy heard the news. He immediately sent me a note and asked me to press pause until we had talked about rehiring this person. For Andy to dip into the organization at this level of decision-making was uncommon. Right away, I knew something bothered him about the idea of hiring this person back on staff.

Quite honestly, I was a little frustrated that he would involve himself in what I considered a mundane matter. This wasn't something that would directly affect him, and I had to work hard not to take the bait on my negative emotions. I had to choose to believe instead that Andy had our best interests in mind. I took some time alone to work through my own emotions and finally was able to sit down with Andy to discuss the matter.

When we spoke, I could tell he had done a lot of personal inspection. He practices the habits of listening to, naming, and questioning his emotions with great regularity and has a high level of self-awareness, and these "invisible" choices have clearly led to visible results over the years. So I wasn't surprised that he had worked through his emotions.

Andy told me how he still hears the voices of his previous bosses in his head whenever someone leaves. *"Wish them luck but keep moving forward, fixated on the future."* He recognized that every situation is different, and that just because someone leaves doesn't mean we should avoid rehiring them. If the person is talented and left on a good note, there's no reason we shouldn't rehire them. Andy had a few specific questions about the situation, and then he gave us permission to move ahead with the hire. He was apologetic for the delay.

I was impressed that day because I saw firsthand how a great leader had made a series of invisible internal decisions, processing through his emotions and asking good questions of himself, to enable him to make wise external decisions. And I knew this was something he did regularly, on a daily basis, and it facilitated his personal development and growth.

In the next few chapters, I want to get practical. To this point, I've been working to give you a vision for why this matters. I hope I've convinced you. But as with anything, the real buy-in happens when you begin to practice the habits. So in the next four chapters, I'm going to introduce you to the key habits you need to integrate into your life.

Here is your warning. No one will praise you for making these invisible decisions. In fact, if you do carry out the habits correctly, others probably won't even notice you're practicing them. These are the behaviors and habits that will allow you to turn down the white noise on a regular basis and help you grow toward greater emotional health.

CHAPTER 6

HABIT ONE:
FINDING
SIMPLICITY

When was the last time you watched a Pixar movie? Because we have little kids, I feel like all we watch are animated movies. Even though I've seen all of them seventeen times, something about those movies always gets to me. I'm not embarrassed to say I cried during *Toy Story 3* . . . and during *Up* . . . and once again during *Inside Out*. They pull on my heartstrings! The people behind those movies know something about telling stories that works, plain and simple.

It has to do with simplicity. While Pixar movies are wildly creative and inventive every time, they're also simple. They ask and answer simple questions. What if toys were actually alive? What will someone do to fulfill their lifelong goal? What if our feelings were people in our heads? These basic springboards are what catapult Pixar movies into such incredible stories.

Andrew Stanton is the Oscar-winning filmmaker behind many of Pixar's classics. In his TED Talk titled "The Clues to a Great Story," he talks about the importance of simplicity when it comes to creating a compelling character: "All well-drawn characters have a spine. And the idea is that the character has an inner motor, a dominant, unconscious goal that they're striving for, an itch they can't scratch. . . . WALL-E's was to find the beauty. Marlin's, the father in *Finding Nemo*, was to prevent harm. And Woody's was to do what was best for his child."[1]

The same is true for you and me. We have a spine. We have something that drives us. It can be a set of values or a way of seeing the world. It can be a goal we want to reach or a person we want to appease. Deep within all of us, something pushes us to do the things we do and to behave the way we behave. Like an engine propels a car forward, so that motivation drives what we do. It's actually quite simple.

If your goal in reading this book is to learn how to lead yourself, this is probably the best place to start. Find that one sentence that defines why you do the things you do, and it can have massive repercussions on your life moving forward. When you can clarify your *why*—and by that, I mean the answer to every "why do you do what you do" question—you can start to live and lead effectively. Finding the why will help you find the traction in life that builds momentum, and it will keep you from being pulled away by distractions.

You probably know that Michael Jordan—the best basketball player ever to play the game (sorry, LeBron)—was cut from his high school basketball team as a sophomore. Later on, he said that whenever he was working out and felt tired or wanted to stop, he would close his eyes and think about the list of varsity basketball players hanging in the school locker room without his name on it. And that was what got him going again.

This chapter is not a lesson in trying harder. It's not about remembering your failures and using them as motivation. It's about knowing your *why*. For Michael Jordan, that list in the locker room was the tangible reminder that he wanted to be the best. He wanted to play basketball at the next level. That was his why, his motivating force, or his "spine," as Andrew Stanton would say.

So what's your spine? What's driving you? Whether you know it or not right now, that question has an answer. Something inside you is pushing you to be the person you are—even if it takes asking some good questions of yourself to figure that out.

In Andrew Stanton's TED Talk, he argues that we all have "spines" that are unchangeable and ultimately out of our control. He says we are wired a certain way, and that wiring is what makes us tick, and we can't do anything about it. This is where he and I disagree.

Human beings are not robots. You are made of flesh and bone. You have desires and ambitions. And you have the power to change and choose. The ancient prophet Isaiah uses an interesting metaphor to describe how we were created:

> But now, O LORD, you are our Father;
> we are the clay, and you are our potter;
> we are all the work of your hand. (Isaiah 64:8 ESV)

Did you catch that? *We are the clay.* I'm no artist, but I've broken out the Play-Doh with my kids before, and I know it's meant to be molded and shaped into different forms. God has not wired you for one single, repetitive task. He is molding you *for* something, but you are not a robot following a computer code. You are a work of art, a malleable being created to change and be changed.

Have you gotten on board with Marie Kondo yet? I heard about her for a few years before I actually gave her show, *Tidying Up with Marie Kondo*, a shot. She mesmerizes my entire family now and I can't explain it. Somehow, she has bumped into a *why* that seems to speak to millions of people: joy. Obviously, within each one of us is a deep desire to find joy. So in her process for "tidying up," she has people pull all their stuff out of the closet, make a large pile, and go through each item one at a time. She has them hold up the item and ask one simple question: "Does this spark joy?"

I kid you not, my kids will walk into the pantry now, pick up a box of cereal, and ask, "Does this spark joy?" I'm a preacher for a living and I've been preaching to my kids their entire lives, but this petite Japanese woman who speaks barely any English barges into our family and does more to help our kids find their why than anything I've ever done. No, I'm not mad. I'm just venting.

Look, you don't have to be Marie Kondo to do this well. We are all born with certain predispositions and grow up with instilled behavioral patterns, but these things can change and adjust based on what we want out of life. Being born into a certain type of family doesn't necessitate that you will raise the same kind of family yourself. Of course, if you are unaware of the habits and patterns and emotions shaping your life, you may end up repeating the mistakes of the past. That's one key reason we need to grow in our emotional awareness. But the good news is that you *can* learn and grow and change and adapt. And today may be your chance to start doing that.

The next section of this chapter is about simplifying your habits and your lifestyle, but you can't do this without simplifying *you*. You won't know which habits and work strategies are important or effective if you don't know the goal toward which they are aimed. Good leaders know three things: where they're coming from, where they're going, and how they're going to get there. The discipline of simplicity takes a look at the first of those things: where you're coming from.

So here are some questions to get you started. What is your driving sentence? What are your essentials? What is your "spine"? What is the varsity basketball roster that reminds you where you came from and why you're going somewhere else? What is your why?

Those aren't easy questions to answer. I don't expect you to answer them right now while you are reading this. And there's a chance that even when you do have an answer, you won't like it. Don't let that frustrate you. Once you define what drives the way you lead and live, you will have a filter for determining which distractions you can do without.

CLEANING OUT YOUR CLOSET

Mark Zuckerberg has only one shirt.

Okay, that's not exactly true. Mark Zuckerberg has multiple versions of one shirt. Do a quick Google Image search of Mark Zuckerberg, and you'll see that when he's not wearing a suit, he is almost always in a plain gray T-shirt. That's kind of weird, right? I mean, the guy invented Facebook. You'd think he has the type of money that would let him buy pretty much any kind of shirt he wants. Scratch that—he has the type of money to buy pretty much any kind of shirt *company* he wants.

But apparently, he wears the same shirt on purpose. In an

interview, Zuckerberg was asked why he always wears the same thing. He responded, "I really want to clear my life so that I have to make as few decisions as possible about anything except how to best serve this community."[2] As much as I may want to make fun of the single-shirt idea, there's something to that.

For starters, Zuckerberg knows his why. He knows his job is to best serve his community. Look at how simple he's made it. Four words: "best serve this community." And once he simplified his why, he looked at his life (or actually, his closet) and started simplifying everything down to the things that support his why. And for him, choosing what to wear every day didn't support his why, so away it went.

I'll have to admit that I spend a considerable amount of time every day wading through my closet and rifling through my dresser drawers—not to mention standing in front of the mirror only to realize my shirt is on inside out. And even if you're someone who gets dressed quickly, that time adds up. Think about it.

Say it takes you five minutes to get dressed in the morning. It takes me about ten minutes for each kid I have to dress, but I'll give you the benefit of the doubt. That means you're spending twenty-five minutes a week getting dressed (assuming you're staying in your pajamas all weekend). Multiply that by the fifty-two weeks in a year and you're spending thirteen hundred minutes a year putting on clothes. That's twenty-one hours—almost a full day!

Now, I'm not saying you need to get rid of every shirt you own except for one color, but Mark Zuckerberg is a good example of how to turn the concept of simplicity into practical, day-to-day habits and decisions. Our lives become more streamlined when we make decisions to simplify. And that simplicity brings clarity and focus.

Have you ever stood in front of your closet and felt completely overwhelmed? Different shirts, jackets, and pants are all hanging there or folded in piles, and you have no idea what to wear. You're meeting your in-laws for dinner and the suit from your wedding looks too formal, but you know your old college T-shirt isn't going to cut it either. So you flick through two or three button-downs—pausing momentarily to wonder where you got the one with pearl-snap buttons and a holographic tiger on the back—before asking your spouse for help.

Simplicity brings clarity.

Now, think about Mark Zuckerberg's closet. When he looks at his closet, he can instantly see all his options. I imagine ten identical T-shirts are hanging up and a few pairs of folded jeans are sitting next to them. That's it. What he's going to wear is overwhelmingly obvious.

To most of us, this whole idea of a simple closet sounds boring, but we can't argue with the fact that simplicity brings clarity. Where you and I have dozens of outfits to choose from, Mark Zuckerberg pulls a shirt off the hanger without looking twice. Simplicity brings clarity.

But how does this apply to your life? I'm not encouraging you to get rid of all your clothes. This metaphor, however, can be super helpful when we think about our lives as our closets. Because if we're honest, most of our lives are crammed full of stuff, maybe even to the point where we can't open the door without things falling out. So I want us to answer some questions.

What are the things you no longer need?

What can you afford to get rid of?

What are the things keeping you from what matters most?

And how can you organize your life like a closet—where you know exactly what you're looking for and you see what matters right away?

Really, what you want to know is this: What is your gray shirt? Better yet, what are your essentials? And remember, the answers to these questions will stem from your answer to the earlier question: What is your why?

Mark Zuckerberg didn't start by cleaning out his closet. He first took the time to simplify why he did what he did, and once he understood his why, he took action to focus only on the things that mattered. That's what we want to do here.

PUTTING THE WHAT WITH THE WHY

So how do we determine our essentials? If we've correctly understood our why, how can we start prioritizing the things that support it? For starters, we're going to look at what's important.

The distinction between important and urgent comes from something known as Dwight D. Eisenhower's decision matrix. Eisenhower is famously known to have said, "What is important is seldom urgent and what is urgent is seldom important."[3] He was making the point that many of us spend our time jumping from one urgent task to another without getting to the important ones. This distinction sounds like an easy enough idea, but most of us do exactly what Eisenhower observed.

I can't tell you the number of times I've chosen to answer emails, texts, and phone calls instead of working on a sermon I was supposed to give in a few days. Now, there's nothing inherently wrong with answering emails and texts. If that's part of your job, you actually have to do those things. The problem occurs when we consistently choose those things over the big, overarching tasks we've been given.

In an ideal world, the urgent tasks should support the important one. But that's almost never the case. Instead, most urgent tasks block us from the important one—at best, they give us the ability to do important things without actually helping us along the way.

We know that simplicity brings clarity, and the same is true the other way around. When we clarify what's important, we can simplify our lives. If my why is to lead people into a growing relationship with Jesus Christ, then anything I do that falls under that main goal is important. Preaching, spending time with people, and leading meetings are important things. I have dozens of managerial tasks I still need to do, but those are urgent, not important. Those things need to get done, but they don't need to control my day.

The same is true for you. If you're the CEO of your company, your why may be to make a profit in your industry. That's important to you, so anything that falls under that idea has to happen. If you're a student, your why is to learn and grow. Anything that helps you learn and grow is important. If you're a stay-at-home mom, your why might be to create resourcefulness and responsibility in your kids. So that extra trip to school to bring in the homework that your son forgot might be something worth eliminating. See how intricately related these two things are? What we do cannot be separated from why we do it, and vice versa.

Not only are the two things inseparable, but they actually grow in strength and meaning when they're combined. We've all worked jobs that we hated. The first job I took in graduate school was working on the first floor of an office building. I was the security. I had no gun. I don't know jiu-jitsu. And I haven't been in a fight since tenth grade (when this kid, whom everyone called Muffy, and I went at it after basketball practice—and nothing about our scuffle made anyone think I should be a UFC fighter). While I grew to love the people who worked in this building, the day-to-day tasks the job required didn't make me leap out of bed in the morning. There were two different things I had to do within the first month of working there.

First, I had to learn the names of the people who worked in this organization. This helped me learn to build a relationship with people when I had nothing to offer them, except some semblance of security they must've felt because I was sitting there keeping watch. Even though learning everyone's name was a small task, I learned from my boss at the time that it mattered. It was a reflection of the larger culture of the organization.

Now, just because the task mattered didn't make it super exciting, but my boss did something helpful—he took a job that seemed fairly menial and gave me a why. He told me why I was doing what I was doing and why it mattered to the overall success of the company. And believe it or not, that simple why made me more eager to show up every day! Knowing that I was supporting the overall goal of the organization and, more specifically, some personal goals set by my boss, gave me a sense of value and purpose every day.

But consider the other task assigned to my job. One of the

other people in charge at this company emailed me after I'd been there a few weeks and asked me to do some data entry for him. I realize some of you reading this may love data entry, but I'm convinced that data entry is inherently boring. It's simply taking numbers and names from one thing and typing them into another. I responded to his email with all the eagerness of someone looking to work their way out of building security. Of course! I'd be happy to help.

When I got to work the next day, a stack of papers was sitting on my desk. That was it. And more papers followed, day after day. I was able to figure out what I needed to do, but there was no explanation for why this work needed to be done. Guess which task I was more excited to get to every day? The one for which I knew the why!

Here's the thing: I'm sure both of those tasks were important in some way—both mattered. But I was motivated to do the one where I knew the purpose, because giving a task a why gives it meaning, and that meaning is empowering. When you know your why, your what becomes more impactful because you're walking in your purpose.

We've already talked about the importance of knowing your personal why—your "spine" or the big-picture purpose behind everything you do. But out of that larger why, many smaller whys give meaning and purpose to the smaller roles you play in life. And understanding those smaller whys will help you simplify your life down to the important and essential things you should be doing. Your life will always hold some tension between accomplishing what's important (but not urgent) and being tempted to focus on doing what's immediate and urgent.

What's important—your why—will vary depending on your

job, your role, your age, and a host of other factors. The truth is that only you know what's most important to you. And what's important to you may have nothing to do with your employment. Maybe you care about making people feel comfortable and welcome. Well, if you're an accountant, your job may not always facilitate this goal. So if you want to find joy in your career and lasting purpose in your day-to-day job, you'll need to find a way to incorporate this goal into your work.

Here's my challenge to you: Simplify what's important to you in each aspect of your life. Try to make your main goal one sentence.

- As an employer, I believe it's important that my company creates a good product.
- As a husband or wife, I believe it's important that my family knows they're cared for.
- As a student, I believe it's important that what I learn today prepares me for my career tomorrow.
- As a Christian, I believe it's important that people around me hear Jesus' name.
- As a sibling, I believe it's important that my family members know I love them.

Simplicity boils down to knowing why you do what you do. You can't clean out your closet until you know why you're doing it. The why becomes your filter for making the tough decisions of what to do and what to drop, what to keep and what to give away.

Let's do a quick recap. Start by understanding your personal why—your "spine" or your driving sentence. Then look at

The truth
is that only
you know
what's most
important
to you.

your professional why—the reason behind your daily tasks and goals. When you clarify your why, you will have a filter you can use to simplify your life. This filter won't magically make those normal, boring day-to-day tasks go away. There will still be phone calls and emails and that one day a week when you have to take out the trash, clean the garage, mow the lawn, and cook dinner. Those things still need to happen. But when you've clarified your why, you can see these things in a new light, through the lens of how they support what ultimately matters.

THE MOOSE AND THE MONKEYS

I want to end this chapter with something I hope you find super practical, because if you're like me, the philosophical "understanding your why" sounds a little frustrating and time-consuming. Just tell me what to do, right? I don't expect you to read this chapter and suddenly have a revelation as to your purpose in life. It will take time and effort to know why you do what you do. But while you spend your lifetime processing all that, here's how you can take simple steps to begin simplifying your life.

It has to do with moose and monkeys. Stay with me here.

Start by making a list of everything you did yesterday. Think of this as your to-do list, except it's actually a to-done list. Put everything on there, even the things that didn't necessarily need to get done. You went to the grocery store, had a lunch meeting, picked up the kids from school, washed the car, watched a movie, brushed your teeth, etc. Put it all on there, but do it as fast as you can. Try to limit yourself to one or two minutes.

Now that you've created the list, circle the things that moved you forward personally or professionally. These are the big things. Maybe you closed a deal, finished a presentation, or ran a mile. They don't necessarily have to be "big"—just circle the things that you look back on and are proud of accomplishing. Maybe you're thinking, *Well, there's nothing like that on my list.* That's okay. Write down something you wish you had done and circle that instead.

The tasks you've circled we'll call *moose*. And the tasks you accomplished but didn't circle we'll call *monkeys*. I'm going to show you how you can chase these things.

Monkeys

If you are a parent, you've probably had a day when you awakened to the sound of children in the kitchen. You walked in and low and behold, your kids had decided to cook themselves breakfast. And by cook, I mean make cereal. And by make cereal, I mean pour milk and cereal all over the counter and the floor.

This isn't how you wanted to start the day, but okay, it is what it is. You clean up the mess, get them fed, get them dressed, and get them out the door. You arrive at work, but you're late. You scramble into the meeting in complete shambles and play catch-up with whatever it is you're talking about that day. Then you leave the meeting and spend the rest of the morning answering emails that you didn't get to yesterday. You realize you're falling behind on the day, so you eat lunch quickly and then get back to your desk.

Suddenly, it's 1:07 p.m. and you can't remember what you were even hoping to get done today. So you spend the next few hours at work trying to catch up on all the managerial tasks you've forgotten, and a few hours later you're on your way home. When you get back, your spouse oh so kindly asks, "How was work today?" and for the life of you, you can't even remember a single thing you accomplished.

Been there? That's a picture of a day spent chasing monkeys.[4]

The monkeys are the smaller, less significant tasks that come up throughout the day. They're the urgent things that aren't inherently "bad"—they're just things that take up time and energy. For example, putting gas in your car can be a monkey. It's something you have to get done, but it's not necessarily something that will move you forward toward your greater goals (unless you work as an Uber driver, in which case it's an important task). Answering emails can be another monkey. Again, it has to happen, but it's not something that makes you feel super accomplished when it's done.

Much like chasing actual monkeys, these tasks feel elusive and frustrating and often take more energy to do than we feel they should. Or they don't feel as rewarding as we want them to.

What you want to hear is me saying, "Forget your monkeys! Don't let those little things get in your way!" Unfortunately, no. I'm not here to tell you to shirk your monkeys. You still need to put gas in your car and answer emails. Those things have to happen. But you need to look at these tasks with a different perspective.

The problem isn't the monkeys themselves. It's that they feel like they divert us from achieving our big-picture goals. So what do we do? We *simplify*.

First, stop chasing monkeys that don't need chasing. You know what these tasks are. Most likely, they're things that need to be delegated to others. If you're a middle manager still filling out everyone's expense reports, you're chasing monkeys. If your job is crunching numbers, but you find yourself leading creative meetings, reevaluate your position. Delegate those things that don't support your why to other people, if you can.

Of course, we all have aspects of our jobs that we don't necessarily want to do. But some of those things, although they are monkeys, still need to be done by us. So here's the second strategy: *batch and catch*. Instead of letting one monkey derail your day, think about how you can put all your monkeys together and view them as a moose (I'll show you what a moose looks like in a moment). Instead of letting little tasks take you away from your big goals, save all your little tasks for one day and turn that batch of tasks into one big goal.

For you, this might look like saving all your monkeys for one day of the week. You can use that day to catch up on all the monkeys you've ignored. The reason this strategy is so helpful is because catching monkeys individually is unfulfilling—those are the days that feel unproductive even though you did a lot. And many of us are stuck in days like this, where we accomplish a lot but feel as though we've done nothing at all.

As we learn to simplify our lives, we should see days like that becoming few and far between. When we get rid of the things that don't support our why, we're more apt to focus our time and energy on what's important—our moose.

Moose

Your moose are your top priorities. In an ideal world, attending to your moose is all you would do with your day. Like we mentioned earlier, these are the important things that help you reach your ultimate goal. They're the tasks that support your spine—the reason you are doing your job and living your life.

When you catch (accomplish) a moose, it feels like a big weight off your chest. Days when you get the big things done are days when you can go home and breathe easy. A lot of us, however, feel like we have fifteen moose. And if you're like me, you probably got frustrated reading about monkeys. You were thinking, *He doesn't understand—little tasks aren't my problem. I have a dozen important things I have to do every day!*

Maybe you do. I'm almost positive you do. We all have important things that need to get done. But the problem is we stretch ourselves too thin by trying to accomplish ten big things every day. And when we do this, we almost never hit our goals and almost always go home frustrated. So what do we need to do? You guessed it: simplify.

Simplify your day. Pick three moose *at most* and catch those today. When it comes to your important tasks, take the exact opposite approach you take with your urgent tasks. We just said that catching monkeys is best when you do all of them at once. The opposite is true for moose. Take them one at a time and pace yourself.

See how this metaphor starts to make sense? If someone tasked you with catching a real-life moose—which is an admittedly bizarre task—would you try to catch ten moose? Of course not! One is overwhelming as it is.

But think about how you would feel if you tried to catch ten but caught only one. You'd be frustrated, defeated, and exhausted. In contrast, if you had realistic expectations and focused on catching one moose at a time, showing up at home with a moose in tow would make for a great day!

That's how we need to start looking at our tasks. Break them down into urgent (monkeys) and important (moose), and treat them accordingly.

This simplified approach to life will relieve you of the burden of trying to do too much, and it will also clarify where you're going—because simplicity brings clarity.

CHAPTER 7

HABIT TWO:
SPEAKING
TO YOURSELF

If simplicity is about finding your *why*, then self-talk is about finding your *way*. If the last chapter was about packing your bags and opening your map, this chapter is about getting in the car and turning out of the driveway. And as with all travels, the destination you desire will determine the direction you choose. If you haven't defined your why, then finding your way won't make sense.

The rampant noise in life demands that we understand this. The distractions in your life will constantly fight to keep you from both your why and your way. We all know this because we've all been overwhelmed before. We've all had days when we didn't have a chance to think about why we were doing things—we were simply acting and behaving in the best, quickest way we knew.

The goal of the habits presented in chapters 6–9 is to remind you of the behaviors you can turn to when the distractions of life are overwhelming. Remember those noise-canceling headphones from chapter 5? They serve as noise filters, allowing you to choose which voices to let in and which to filter out. At different times and in different situations, these habits are specific and dependable tools to create space for you to interrogate your emotions.

The irony of self-talk is that, if it's not understood and used correctly, it can incidentally add to the noise. You're talking to yourself all day long. And the messages you're giving yourself are not always trustworthy. That's why we're going to

The destination you desire will determine the direction you choose.

take some time to understand and unpack that voice inside our heads. And we're going to see how employing the habit of self-talk will help you find your way toward becoming the leader you know you can be.

In the movie *Stranger Than Fiction*, Will Ferrell plays Harold Crick—an IRS agent with a humdrum life that is suddenly turned completely upside down when he starts hearing a voice inside his head narrating his every move. As it turns out, this voice belongs to Karen Eiffel, played by Emma Thompson, who is an award-winning novelist working on her next book. From Karen's perspective, Harold Crick is simply a character in her book. From Harold Crick's perspective, Karen Eiffel is narrating his very life.

The movie is pretty hilarious. As we watch Harold's life narrated by the voice of its author, we see Harold grow first frustrated and then resigned that the voice in his head can predict what he's going to do. By the end of the movie, Harold finally meets and confronts Karen to tell her that it's his life she happens to be writing and, well, I won't ruin the ending for you, but it's worth seeing.

All that to say, this movie shows something about each of our lives. We all have a narrator in our heads. But unlike in the movie *Stranger Than Fiction*, this voice doesn't belong to some outside person watching us live our lives. Instead, it belongs to us. I'm talking about that voice inside your head that's always talking to you. If you're still not sure what I'm talking about, read this sentence very slowly. Now, read this one fast. Now, go back and read the first one fast and the second one slow.

If you did that, you just activated the voice inside your head. That's how you're reading this right now. There's a voice somewhere between your eyes and your brain that is taking the strange markings on this piece of paper and translating them into language and cohesive thoughts. How this works, I have no idea. And I completely understand if you're now totally mind-blown and need to take a break from reading for a while because the whole voice-inside-your-head thing is freaking you out. Set down the book, pace up and down a little, then come on back when you're ready.

You'll notice this voice inside your head commonly shows up in places like the shower. Have you ever come up with a great idea while reading the back of the shampoo bottle? Or maybe you're someone who finds yourself winning arguments inside your mind as you drive to work. That's the voice inside your head again. That's self-talk. All of us do it—but we may not realize how helpful it can be.

Back to the movie *Stranger Than Fiction*. The tension driving the entire movie is that the voice inside Harold Crick's head is out of his control. This voice that he can't control is throwing his life completely out of balance. He understands that the voice in his head has a great deal of power, and when that power belongs to someone other than Harold, the results are nerve-wracking.

The same is true for you and me.

We need to understand that the voice inside our heads has the power to directly affect how we live our lives. But unlike Harold Crick's predicament, that voice inside our heads belongs to us, and that means you and I have the power to control how it affects us.

THE VOICE OF POWER

Have you ever found yourself scrolling through your Instagram feed and hopelessly comparing yourself to the people you see there? I don't know what it is about social media, but it sometimes seems like the people on there are from a different planet. Maybe I'm alone on this one, but tell me if any of these people sound familiar.

- The too-tan, too-fit sports-bra-wearing exercise models who have just the butt-busting routine you need to start your morning.
- The world-traveling passport punchers who have as many selfies in front of seafronts as there are grains of sand on the seashore.
- Don't forget the ripped-skinny-jean-wearing, top-button swag, beanie-bopping motivational speakers who absolutely cannot wait to tell you the three keys for living life to the fullest—"Carpe diem, am I right?"

You know, *those* people. I don't have any beef with them, per se. But I know they sometimes make me feel worse about myself. I look at them and think, *I'll never look that good while I'm working out.* Or *I'll never be able to afford that kind of vacation with my family.*

The problem, I think, isn't the people on Instagram. As easy as it is to point fingers at "them" and blame them for bringing out these comparisons and insecurities in me, it's not something they're trying to do (hopefully). I choose to believe that a majority of people on social media don't spend time posting things with the purpose of making other people jealous or self-conscious.

But regardless of whether they mean to do this or not, it's another way the noise around me fuels my negative self-talk. Those Instagram posts lead to harmful, negative thoughts that I dwell on for the rest of the day. If I wake up to a video of a CrossFit guy doing one-armed pull-ups with a weight vest on and three bags of flour tied around his waist, that's going to make me feel a little self-conscious. Next thing I know, I'm not comfortable in my own skin, and that insecurity follows me to work, into meetings, and back home again.

That's how the voice inside your head works. It snowballs the negative things you hear and say throughout your day in powerful ways. But here's the good news: the reverse is true as well.

My wife happens to be a great encourager. And I happen to be a sucker for handwritten notes. The other day, she sent me an email that brought tears to my eyes. (I'm seeing a theme here.) I know what you're thinking, and yes, that's exactly as adorable as it sounds. But guess how I carried myself for the rest of the day? Like a man who had a proud wife supporting him!

You bet I walked around the office with a little extra pep in my step and a little strut in my suit. Because that's what positive self-talk does.

My wife didn't know she was doing this, but what that note did was help me begin my day with uplifting self-talk that carried me forward for the rest of the day, even when meetings didn't go as well as I'd hoped. I had

That voice inside your head has power.

that note in the back of my mind, and the voice inside my head was continually reminding me of it.

That voice inside your head has power. It can control your day by discouraging and demotivating, or it can encourage and empower. The great news is, it's up to you. You are able to control that little voice. Really, you can.

THE POWER OF VOICE

While the voice inside your head has power over you, you also have power over the voice. Most people recognize the first part—we know one negative thought can put a damper on our day while one positive thought can brighten everything—but few of us acknowledge the second half of that truth. And that's what I want us to do—because our lives get better when we learn to filter the noise around us. When we control the noise, we can better control the voice in our heads. And when we limit the negative and let in that which encourages us, our outlook on life will improve.

Start by acknowledging that the voice inside your head is there. It sounds simple because it is. A good example of someone who was excellent at this is David, one of the writers of the biblical psalms, poetry that was often set to music. Look at what he wrote in Psalm 42:5:

> Why, my soul, are you downcast?
>> Why so disturbed within me?
> Put your hope in God,
>> for I will yet praise him,
>>> my Savior and my God.

Notice two things here. First, David was hyper-aware of his inner self. He knew the voice inside his head, and he wasn't afraid to talk back to it. In Psalm 42, we see that he was downcast. Something was wrong or something had upset him. And not only did David know himself well enough to recognize this, but he took the time for some introspection. He paused what he was doing, filtered out the noise, and said to himself, "What's going on here?"

But he didn't stop there. He acknowledged the negative self-talk and did something to change it. He reminded himself of truth, and he reminded himself of what was good. Many of us can realize when something is off. We can recognize when negative self-talk is happening. But we don't always know how to change a pattern of negative self-talk into positive self-talk. Learning this skill has powerful repercussions for our emotional intelligence.

David gives us the key to positive self-talk—reminding ourselves of truth. For David, that truth was found in remembering who God is and why God is the source of hope, obviously a great truth to remind ourselves of every day. We'll also benefit from reminding ourselves of specific truths that counter the lies perpetuated by our negative self-talk. This skill is known as self-regulation.

GETTING INSIDE YOUR HEAD

Not only has Daniel Goleman helped shape much of the learning around the topic of emotional intelligence, he has also been a leading voice on the subject of self-talk. In a recent interview,[1] he discussed how the art of speaking to yourself has become essential for business leaders—to the point where it's now one of the factors that defines a person's success.

An emotionally intelligent person is adept at self-narrating their life. Goleman points out that this is not an unusual skill. It's something we all do to some extent. We all have a voice inside our heads telling us what to do, and whether we're paying attention or not, we're listening to and ignoring that voice at our own discretion. The voice in our heads is often listening to other voices—other people around us, things we read or watch, and even reflections we might have on our experiences or memories. Just considering how many possible voices we let speak inside our heads can be mind-blowing.

Goleman says, "We don't realize how busy our mind is until we stop and look at it. Our mind is wandering all the time."[2] And that's true, isn't it? Your mind is probably wandering right now even as you're reading this. Our minds were created to be active. They want to have information and ideas going in and out of them constantly. Even in the moments when we're doing nothing, our brains are at work. That creates a unique tension. On the one hand, we like to keep our brains busy processing all the things we do and think. But on the other hand, we sense that giving our brains a break is necessary at times. The key here is regulation. We have to make a deliberate choice to serve as the gatekeepers in our own heads—allowing what's good to come in, making sure the unhelpful stays out, and knowing when to give ourselves a break from all the input. We are able to regulate the voice inside our heads to the point where the wanderings and the breaks are beneficial to us.

Self-regulation isn't a new idea. As I mentioned earlier, you're already engaging in self-talk every day. How many times have you come up with a great idea in the shower or just before falling asleep at night? Or won that argument in your head while you're driving? Something about those low-input moments creates extreme clarity and creativity. And those are the moments we want to foster. That's how self-talk works. Self-talk is the means through which you regulate what's going in and out of your brain. It's the way you control the narration so the voice speaking to you adds value and makes you better.

The main way to regulate your inner voice is to filter out the noises that aren't adding value. Whether you're reading books and articles, watching shows and movies, or surfing the web, all these sources are saying things that the voice inside your head is communicating to you. That's a lot of voices and a lot of noise.

Odds are, too much information is coming into your head for you to continuously self-regulate. How are you going to hear the voice inside your head if you're not filtering the voices that are talking? The reason good ideas come to us while we're driving or taking a shower or trying to fall asleep is because those might be the only moments of the day when other voices aren't allowed in. When you're alone, you're alone with the voice inside your head—for better or worse.

You can think about this idea from the opposite perspective too. The flip side of self-talk is to do nothing, right? If we don't try to control or regulate the voices inside our heads, they will simply speak whatever happens to enter. That's how we become like robots. In goes 2 + 2 and out comes 4. Nothing else to it.

What I'm saying is that if we aren't talking to ourselves, other voices are. And if we aren't regulating what's coming in, then we have no reason to expect to control what's going out. Self-talk is happening inside your head whether you like it or not. But you want to make sure your desired self is included in your self-talk. You know the kind of leader you want to be. Self-talk can be the way you remind yourself of your goals, while helping you reach them at the same time.

And the only time you're going to be able to talk to yourself is when no one else is. So it's important to give yourself the time and the space to be alone. Sounds weird, I know. But self-talk happens in places like the shower—places where we're quiet and alone and nothing is trying to take our headspace.

So how do we make this happen? It starts with creating pockets in the day for self-talk. You need to create openings where not too many things are vying for your attention. That's what I want us to turn to now—habits to help make positive self-talk happen.

LEADING YOURSELF ON A MOMENT-BY-MOMENT BASIS

Here's the first habit for fostering positive self-talk: Set up your day the night before. This simple idea makes a big difference.

Remember what we talked about earlier—self-talk snowballs. If the first thing you do in the morning is check your email, add things to your calendar, and mentally go over the meetings you have coming up, you'll be overwhelmed before you get out of bed.

That's when thoughts of *I can't get everything done today* and *I don't have the ability to make this happen* start. And from there you're sucked into a downward spiral of negative self-talk. Plus, when the first thing you do is mentally go through your calendar, you'll already have so many voices inside your head that you'll never have a chance to hear yourself think.

Scheduling your day the night before gives you the power to control your self-talk from the moment you wake up. Instead of logging in the moment you're awake, you can go through a normal routine of brushing your teeth, working out, showering, getting dressed, or whatever it is you do with your mind free. This is the space where you're capable of having a conversation with the voice inside your head. When you know the day has already been taken care of, you have the freedom to take care of yourself before you begin the day.

When you know the day has already been taken care of, you have the freedom to take care of yourself before you begin the day.

Another helpful habit to establish is deciding you're not going to surf the internet or check emails before you complete certain tasks. This goes along with the idea of scheduling your day the night before. Simple things like email and social media can derail your day before it even begins. When you set up your day the night before, choose the one thing—the moose—that has to get done before you let any distractions, or monkeys, into your head. This will keep your head clear of noise, which will help keep your head clear of negative self-talk.

Here are two good questions to ask as you set up your calendar:

1. What is motivating me to say yes to this?
2. Is there someone else who can do this?

These two questions force you to do two things we talked about in the previous chapter. The first question forces you to analyze your why. Why do I want to do this? Why is this something that needs to be on my calendar? Why is this important to me? Most of the time, the answer to this question will be obvious. But in cases when the answer is unclear, you'll get to reevaluate why you're doing certain things. And chances are, this analysis will help you simplify your life and will rid you of certain noises and distractions.

Also, the first question allows you to have a conversation with yourself. And if we know anything about great leaders, it's that they know how to lead themselves. Asking yourself questions is how you do that. Thinking critically and objectively through self-talk will transform, first, the way you lead yourself and, second, the way you lead others.

The second question forces you to think about how you can delegate tasks. This question will help you recognize the tasks that keep you from doing what is important and help you hand them off to someone else. For those of us who have a hard time delegating (you can't see me, but I'm pointing at myself), this question will free us up to pass along more tasks.

Here are two other self-regulating questions you can ask yourself:

1. What would a great leader do here?
2. What advice would I give someone else who was in this situation?

Now, these questions have less to do with our calendars, but asking them of ourselves is a healthy habit to get into. You're training the voice in your head to think critically by giving it a goal. You want to be a great leader one day—at least, I assume that's why you're still reading. It doesn't hurt to remind yourself of that goal every once in a while! Great leaders are always thinking and always asking questions. You may not always know what a great leader would do in your situation, but training yourself to ask the question will open your mind to see the possibility that you behave like a great leader more than you realize.

Great leaders are always thinking and always asking questions.

The other self-regulating question about advice is helpful because it allows you to get outside yourself and objectively analyze your situation. Instead of being frustrated that the meeting you just led went poorly, you can picture someone else in that situation. What would you tell a colleague if they asked you how to respond after failing to lead well in front of

Self-talk will help your days be not only more productive but more positive.

others? You'd probably tell them to brush it off and try again. Boom, there you go. Tell that to yourself and keep going with your day. It's that simple.

If you start your day with positive self-talk and intersperse helpful self-regulating questions throughout the day, then the only thing left is to end with more positive self-talk.

Self-talk will help your days be not only more productive but more positive. And you can focus on this positivity as you wind down your day in a healthy, noise-free way. Instead of turning on your favorite TV show as you fall asleep, or instead of reading that last article online, simply close your eyes and take in how good it feels to have done what you said you were going to do.

There's nothing wrong with resting in an accomplishment-filled day. Plus, it gives you the time to slow down. Watching Netflix and catching up on social media are some of my favorite nighttime activities. But when I compare nights spent entertaining myself to nights where I simply relax and wind down with my wife by my side, the choice is a no-brainer. After I've scheduled my next day, slowing the night down helps me relax and recognize the good things I may have missed throughout the day. Not only do I enjoy a slower nighttime routine, but it helps me sleep better—which then makes the next day better! It's a positive cycle that just keeps going.

And it all starts with self-talk. If you're going to start your day with positivity, it only makes sense to end it the same way.

THE NEW YOU

Honestly, there's a part of me that resists self-talk. Something about the idea seems weird to me. You mean I'm supposed to talk to myself? If I start having conversations with myself, people are going to think I've lost it.

If those thoughts were running through your head as you read this chapter, don't worry. I understand. In fact, I relate to you more than you might think. But what I've learned about self-talk is that it works. The only thing crazier than talking to yourself is not practicing self-talk. So my challenge is this: Try it.

This chapter offers a few practical habits that you can try for yourself right now. Whether or not you're convinced by the whole idea, you won't know if it works if you don't give it a chance. And I'm telling you, in a world that is only growing noisier, the ability to use self-talk for our own benefit is only going to prove more and more valuable.

Give yourself the freedom today to do something that might be a little strange: Talk to yourself. Listen. Slow down and ask self-regulating questions. I promise that if you practice these habits, you'll be taking steps toward being a better leader as well as a better spouse, parent, coworker, sibling, and person.

CHAPTER 8

HABIT THREE: GETTING QUIET

Would you try something before we move on? Silence your phone, turn off the music, and set a timer for two minutes.

Sit silently until the alarm goes off.

I'm happy to wait on you while you try this.

How was that? As I was writing this, I tried it myself and was reminded once again how difficult silence can be.

We are *not* comfortable with silence, but silence is so powerful. Through the team at EmotionallyHealthy.org, I learned of a fascinating example that brings out tremendous emotion in me every single time I watch it.[1] Researchers brought in sets of parents and adult kids to have them experience the power of emotional silence. They were brought into a sterile room, one parent-child pair at a time, and were asked to stand facing each other for four minutes. Perfectly quiet, perfectly still, with no distractions for *four* full minutes. Of course, when NBC aired the project, they didn't show the entire four minutes, but they did show the powerful emotions that rose to the surface simply because of the space provided by silence.

A mother told of how she looked into her son's face and thought about the moment he was born.

A son told of how much gratitude he felt, thinking about how much his mother had sacrificed for him.

A father told of how much potential he saw in his daughter's future.

It's such a simple but profound concept. Why? Because we are not comfortable with silence, yet it is so powerful!

Emotionally healthy leaders turn down the noise low enough and long enough to allow space for curiosity. As difficult or uncomfortable as this might be, it absolutely requires the habit of getting quiet. And it can't be a onetime thing. It must become part of your daily or at the very least weekly routine in life.

Emotionally healthy leaders turn down the noise low enough and long enough to allow space for curiosity.

Silence is scarce. Honestly, it might even be nonexistent. When was the last time you sat in complete silence? Having five little kids has made silence an absolute impossibility. My wife and I have actually contemplated having our kids' hearing checked because they're so loud. Honestly though, I can't make a commute without listening to podcasts or music. Sitting quietly in my car drives me nuts! And that's not because there's anything wrong with silence itself. No, it's because we've never been trained to appreciate silence. For most people, it's an acquired taste.

Appreciating silence is especially difficult when I'm by myself. And those moments are rare given my wiring and personality. Times of solitude are times when I most desire sound. If I make time in the day to go for a run or a walk alone, there's no way I'm going without my phone. I have to have some sort of sound in my head.

My goal in this chapter is to show that many of us are missing out on two crucial habits that can change our lives for the better: silence and solitude. And I think if you give both a try, you'll start to see things differently. You'll appreciate smaller things more and you'll face bigger challenges with more confidence. But don't take my word for it. Let's look at someone who, having more leadership power than anyone who has ever lived, made silence and solitude a regular part of his life.

TIME IS NOT A GREAT EXCUSE

In Mark's account of the life of Jesus, we find his perspective on the beginning of Jesus' ministry. And in only a handful of verses, Mark shows us how crucial silence and solitude were in the life of Jesus. If God incarnate needed silence and solitude, I'd say you and I should pay attention to our own need for these things as well.

Starting in Mark 1:14, Jesus walks into Galilee and starts preaching. He goes throughout the town telling people about the good news he has brought with him. "The kingdom of God is at hand" (1:15 ESV). This is big news! Immediately, people start following him around, trying to hear more. As he traverses the town, Jesus starts calling his disciples. Like Oprah handing out free cars, Jesus points to Simon Peter and says, "You get to follow me!" Then to his brother Andrew, "And you get to follow me!"

They immediately drop what they're doing and follow Jesus. Why not, right? Next time we see them they're at the synagogue. Think of this place as a mix between the town center and the church. It was the Sabbath, so everyone had gathered to hear the teaching. Now, you have to picture this. Those gathered have priests who teach them every week—the same way a church would have a regular pastor giving the message. But suddenly, this complete stranger gets up and starts right in on what he has to say.

Did the priests ask Jesus to teach? Did the people know he was coming? I have no idea. But I can't help but picture Jesus bursting through the doors and walking straight to the front. I don't know if that's exactly how it happened, but regardless, Jesus teaches in a way the people have never heard before.

To me, this is the strangest part of the story. What did he teach? What did he say? I can't imagine! But whatever he said was powerful, because the people were astonished. Then things get even crazier.

While Jesus is teaching, a man with an unclean spirit starts yelling at him. Jesus gets heckled! Again, was this a regular church attendee? Or was this guy new too? We don't know. All we know is that Jesus casts the unclean spirit out of this man. What?

I don't know if you've ever seen comedians roast hecklers—it can be pretty funny—but that's nothing compared to Jesus. This man is yelling at him, and Jesus says, "Be silent, and come out of him!" (Mark 1:25 ESV). And—bam! The spirit leaves. This has already been a big day for Jesus. Even reading about it has me a little exhausted. But wait, there's more!

Jesus leaves the synagogue and goes to the house of Simon's mother-in-law, who happens to be very sick. Can you imagine Jesus coming to your house the one day you're sick in bed? I'm picturing Simon's mother-in-law sniffling with puffy eyes and Kleenex scattered all over the bed (I know Kleenex hadn't been invented yet, but just follow along). This is the scene Jesus walks into. And what does he do? He heals her. Of course.

In an instant she goes from lying in bed to bustling around the house making dinner and serving them. News of this miracle spreads quickly, and people line up outside the house asking Jesus to heal them. Mark tells us that "the whole town gathered at the door" (Mark 1:33). And Jesus heals one after another after another.

Now, I would think that after that type of day, Jesus would probably sleep in. Seems fair, right? Nope. We read, "And rising very early in the morning, while it was still dark, he departed and went out to a desolate place, and there he prayed" (Mark 1:35 ESV).

This story fascinates me. Not only does it paint this incredible picture of Jesus bursting onto the scene, but it also reveals his character in cool and subtle ways. Moreover, it shows us the value of silence and solitude. If Jesus knew and acted on the importance of getting away, getting alone, and getting quiet, shouldn't we?

If Jesus knew and acted on the importance of getting away, getting alone, and getting quiet, shouldn't we?

GETTING AWAY

Just as Jesus moved to a remote place where he could be alone, so we need to create distance between the noise and us.

Now, getting away does not look like buying a "Wanna Get Away" ticket on the next Southwest flight. I'm not suggesting you take solo vacations away from your family. That's a bad idea for me. In fact, if we only make time to get away once every six months for a week at a time, we won't experience the benefits of this habit.

Have you ever gone on a vacation only to return home more tired than you were when you left? This happens one of two ways. One is that you show up hoping for a week of peace and quiet, when in reality you've planned a stay at a Disney resort and you find your schedule packed with activities. Then, somewhere between pictures with Donald Duck and adventures in the Magic Kingdom, you realize you've just traded in the busyness of normal life for the busyness of vacation.

The other way is that you show up for a great week of rest and relaxation, hoping to spend your time sitting on the beach reading a book or lounging by the pool. Then, two days into doing nothing, you realize that laziness isn't restful. Doing nothing can feel great for a little while, but it doesn't do anything for you. Even if you enjoy your full week off, you get back home and the routine you left is suddenly twice as exhausting as you remember. Why? Because you shirked the rhythm of life and the readjustment period only makes you more tired than you were when you left.

My point is that the practice of silence and solitude is not something you do every quarter—it's something you do every week, even every day. In reality, getting away happens on a much smaller scale. Getting away doesn't happen by traveling. Instead, it happens by finding a place you can retreat to every day. Because let's be honest: none of us are monks. At least, I don't think so. We have jobs and families and friends and hobbies and communities that we're a part of—and those are great things! So instead of trying to "escape" from them into a place of isolation, we need to learn how to get away from noise at appropriate times and in a healthy way.

But that doesn't mean we can't learn from monks. Here is what Thomas Merton, the famous monk, writer, and theologian, said about silence and solitude:

> Not all men are called to be hermits, but all men need enough silence and solitude in their lives to enable the deep inner voice of their own true self to be heard at least occasionally. When that inner voice is not heard, when man cannot attain to the spiritual peace that comes from being perfectly at one with his true self, his life is always miserable and exhausting. For he cannot go on happily for long unless he is in contact with the springs of spiritual life which are hidden in the depths of his own soul.[2]

Like Merton said, you don't need to be a hermit. But you do need to find ways to get away, get alone, and get quiet. So how do you start? It's simple: find your place, find your time, and find your practice.

Find Your Place

Even though I don't start every morning the same way, I have grown to love routine. Too often, the first thing I do is grab my phone. I'm trying to break that habit. At this stage of our family, I've learned that with most things, if I don't get it done early, it's not going to get done. So I've learned to long for the early morning to clear my mind and begin with the habits that are healthiest for me.

But I have one constant every morning: my desk. After coffee, my desk is the first place I go in the morning to get my day started. My dad used to fuss at me when I was a kid about keeping a clean desk because it's a microcosm of your mind. Amazing that the older I get, the more right my dad becomes. I usually spend five minutes getting the setting just right and then my morning mind routine begins. In fact, I'm sitting here right now.

I sit at this desk for at least a part of every morning. On good days, I get quality time at this desk. But even on days when I'm rushed, sitting down for even just fifteen minutes is worth it. This is the place I go to get away. It's where I practice silence and solitude. And no matter what your living situation, you need a place. You need a constant location that is free of noise and distraction. What you'll find is that when you designate your place, you'll be able to keep it clear of those things.

The cool part about this is that you can make your place your own. As I've lived in different houses, dorms, and apartments through the different stages of life, I've had different places for silence and solitude. The kitchen table, a desk in my room, and a couch in my office have all served as my place. Heck, there was a time when the kids were young that the toilet was my place. Sometimes you gotta do what you gotta do to get away!

Your place doesn't have to be anything special. It doesn't

need to have soundproof walls. It doesn't need to be a secret location that only you know. It just has to be a place dedicated to noise-free reflection. It has to be a place where you've decided that the distractions of the world can't touch you. And it has to be a place you can return to regularly.

Find Your Time

The idea of returning regularly is key to the practice of silence and solitude. This is why "your place" can't be the beach house your family visits every summer. That's not how it works. Your place needs to be somewhere you can go every day, and the way you instill this habit is by picking a time to practice it.

Most people prefer mornings, and personally, I'm one of those people. If I can manage to stay away from email, the news, and social media in the morning, I can see the positive effect that has on my mindset for the remainder of the day. Something about starting the day in slow silence allows me to pray and prepare for what's ahead. It allows me to clear my mind of any clutter and get ready for whatever the day will bring.

I don't think you have to choose early mornings. Obviously, you need to find a time that works for you. People are usually either morning larks or night owls. And just so you know, even though most of us don't begin that way, the research says we're all headed toward becoming morning larks. Researchers have found that only 7 percent of young adults are morning larks. But by age 60, only 7 percent of people are *still* night owls. Also, morning larks tended to say they felt happier than night owls.[3] Though you may feel hardwired to be a night owl, you might be able to trick yourself into becoming more of a morning person.

Personally, I think the benefits of morning outweigh the benefits of other times of the day. But whether you practice silence and solitude in the morning, throughout the day, or at night, you can't do it without intentionality. Choose the time that works best with your schedule and your personality. If you're an angry morning person, don't wake up at 5:00 a.m. to sit in silence for two hours. You won't enjoy it, nor will you get anything out of it. If you know that most of your meetings happen before lunch, don't try to squeeze thirty minutes of silence somewhere they won't fit.

> Whether you practice silence and solitude in the morning, throughout the day, or at night, you can't do it without intentionality.

Again, the key here is consistency. Even though you can find people who will tell you they can find silence and solitude at night, I've rarely met a successful person who lets the sun beat them up. Do your own research, though. Make the question of morning routine one of the questions you ask successful people. The bottom line: the habits of silence and solitude depend entirely on regularity. Don't pick a time that you don't like or that you don't think will work. As Russell Westbrook says in that Mountain Dew commercial, "Don't do they. Do you." Then, when you've set a place and time, you can start your practice.

Find Your Practice

If you haven't noticed, the theme of these two habits is *you*. Silence and solitude can look different for every single person.

There's no one place, one time, or one way to practice these habits. You simply have to find what works best for you and commit yourself to following through.

My practice looks fairly basic. I like my desk in the mornings. First, I read the Bible, journal, and pray. Normally, this takes about thirty minutes and allows me to get my heart in a teachable place. Second, I write down a few things I'm grateful for. Problems dim in the light of gratitude. I've also found that gratitude snaps me out of the future and back into the now. This takes less than five minutes. And third, I look through my day to think about how to make the meetings I have more productive. I use the question, "What does this person need from me?" as a way to jog my thoughts toward others. I spend about twenty minutes on this step. Altogether, I try to spend one hour in silence and solitude.

My brother-in-law, on the other hand, has an entirely different strategy. See, he's kind of a freak athlete. He does triathlons, which means he's in crazy good shape and spends a lot of time training. For someone like him, sitting still for half an hour doesn't work. So he practices silence and solitude on his bike. Whether he's riding on a trail or on the road, or even at home on his trainer, his bike seat is his place.

Personally, I can't think of anything worse. But for him, he finds that the best time to be alone with his thoughts is while he's working out. Maybe you're that way too. Maybe going for a run in the morning without headphones is the best way for you to experience silence and solitude. Maybe you like the idea of sitting, but you don't want to read or write. How about drawing something? Or doing absolutely nothing but meditating on your day?

I have a friend who likes to golf. So for his practice of silence and solitude, he puts a mug on the floor and putts golf balls into it for ten to twenty minutes every night before he goes to bed. See how creative you can be with this practice? Figure out the habits and rituals that suit you best and make them a part of your routine.

The point is, *it's up to you!* Your place, your time, your practice. But I know what you're thinking: *I need more direction.* Me too. That's why we're going to turn to the idea of getting alone and why and how solitude will affect your well-being.

GETTING ALONE

The problem with noise is that it constantly bombards us with other voices. Whether you're dealing with a boatload of emails or scrolling through social media, the voices of other people are constantly there. And in one sense, this can be a good thing. Staying informed and communicating with others are both healthy and important facets of life. But if we never get a break to be by ourselves, we'll never learn to think. And if we can't think, we can't lead.

Still, this is how many of us operate. Next time you're in a doctor's office or you're in line waiting for something, look around you. How many people are staring at their phones? I'll be the first to admit that I do this. Anytime I find myself with a moment of free alone time, I pull out my phone. Half the time, I don't even realize what I'm doing. It's a reflex. Theologian, professor, and author Donald Whitney writes: "Culture conditions us to be comfortable with noise and crowds, not with silence and solitude, and to feel more at home in a mall than at a park."[4]

Does that sound true for you? So many of us are uncomfortable with the silence that solitude brings. Which means few of us are naturally prepared to practice this habit. We've trained our minds and bodies to be constantly surrounded by the noise of others. As a result, getting alone is going to take practice. It's going to feel strange at first, maybe downright unnatural. But in the same way that self-talk helps us better understand the voice inside our heads, so getting alone will help us know ourselves better.

If you want to be a good leader, knowing who you are and what you're about is crucial. Followers naturally become like their leaders. Think about it. Apple took on the personality of Steve Jobs. The values of Amazon reflect the values of Jeff Bezos. Every company, corporation, and community reflects the person leading it. But if you don't understand yourself and your values, how are you going to lead others? How can you expect the people who follow you to know what you're about if you don't know yourself?

The startling truth is that few of us really know ourselves, and even fewer of us are taking the time to try to learn. C. H. Spurgeon made this exact same observation over one hundred years ago: "Few men truly know themselves as they really are."[5]

You can't get to know yourself as you really are if you don't make time to step away from the noise and be alone. Solitude means being alone with yourself long enough to learn who you are.

This isn't easy—especially if you're a people person like

If you want
to be a good
leader, knowing
who you are
and what
you're about is
crucial.

I am. Solitude will be extraordinarily helpful for your overall well-being, but it can also create some serious FOMO (for my parents: that means Fear of Missing Out). So let's look at how to make getting alone a high priority and a good practice.

Start Small

If you've never practiced solitude, spending an entire weekend completely alone may not be the best first step. It certainly isn't the best way to build a habit. If you're training for a marathon, your first workout shouldn't be a fifteen-mile run. Instead, you should start small.

Practice solitude in five- or ten-minute installments once a day for a few weeks. That's it. Maybe that means waking up five minutes early or going on a short stroll during your lunch break. Whatever it is, make it small and manageable. When you start to form a habit, you want the first step to feel doable. Spending five minutes alone, without noise or distractions, is something you can definitely do today. There's no pressure to perform or do anything out of the ordinary. I'm not even saying you need to try to accomplish anything in those five minutes— you shouldn't try to accomplish anything.

I've found success practicing short times of solitude in my car. When I first started to implement this habit, the idea of silence and solitude annoyed me. I have friends who have done a daylong stay at a monastery. To me that sounds like running a marathon without any training. Beginning with only a few minutes of silence in my car allowed me to stretch my solitude muscle. It helped me realize that the first few minutes of the day belong to me. Now I use them to think about whatever I want. There's no agenda, no priority, nothing that needs to get accomplished. I simply get to be alone with my thoughts. I think it's worth it, but you'll need to decide that for yourself.

Start Slow

One of the great benefits of solitude is that it helps me slow down. That's why I'm a fan of practicing it at the beginning of the day. If you're like me, once the day gets going, it can be difficult to stop. The rhythms of life move quickly, and we can easily find ourselves falling behind.

But solitude slows me down. It keeps me from getting overwhelmed. And that's what I mean by starting slow. As you first incorporate this habit into your life, don't give yourself too much to do in your time alone. The temptation will be to think through a certain number of things. Maybe you'll want to remind yourself of your personal goals, or maybe you'll run through your schedule for the day in your head, making sure you're prepared for every meeting. That's not what solitude is for.

Away from the high speeds of the world, solitude is a place of safety. If you enter into a place of solitude with an agenda, you won't find rest or peace. So resist the desire to do something or to get something done. Sit with your thoughts and slow down. Everything that has to happen will still be there in five minutes. You can afford the time it takes to go slow.

Stay Strong

Spoiler alert: The habit of solitude won't always reap instant benefits. You might even practice solitude for weeks at a time with no tangible benefits. If someone were to ask you why you took the time to be alone, you might not have an answer right away. That's okay.

Solitude offers great relief and great frustration. On one hand, you don't have to "get anything out of it." On the other hand, sometimes there is nothing to "get out of it." If you're a high achiever, this will be a frustrating paradigm. But that's exactly something you should lean into. Part of the noise of the world is an unspoken pressure to perform and to achieve. Solitude is an inherent rebuttal of that noise.

There's nothing to achieve—no accomplishment to show at the end of five minutes alone. The benefits are entirely internal and often unfelt. Stick with it. The practice of solitude takes time, but it's worth the consistency. You're practicing something that is completely against cultural norms. The noise of the world doesn't want you to hear yourself. I promise that every day you'll be able to think of something better to do with five minutes than spending it in solitude and silence. But practicing these habits will free you to be a better leader, someone who isn't constantly drowning in the same noise that everyone else hears.

GETTING QUIET

Once you learn to get away and get alone, all that's left is to get quiet. This is the most challenging part. This is so hard that it's one of the driving reasons behind the writing of this book. But you can do three things to make this step easier and more rewarding.

Shut Up

In the last chapter we looked at self-talk and the importance of conversing with our internal voice. And often you can use solitude to do just that. But there's also something helpful about shutting up and listening.

As you begin, you might find that you need something to guide your thoughts. If so, I routinely go back to these two prayer-like formats.

1. Heavenly Father, what do you want *for me* today?
   I want . . .
   I need . . .
2. I surrender . . .

My mind is always going a thousand miles a minute, and getting quiet doesn't happen naturally. But when it does happen, it refreshes me in a way that no other habit does. I bet you've already experienced something like this.

Have you ever been driving a route that you knew super well and suddenly arrived at your destination without any recollection of the drive? Sounds dangerous, I know. But maybe your commute home is so familiar that you don't think about the turns you're making or the roads you're on. You just drive on autopilot. Then you show up in your driveway and feel like you're waking up from a trance.

That's the type of feeling that shutting up will help you experience. It's easy to "practice" silence and solitude when, in reality, all you're doing is talking to yourself or thinking out loud. Truly getting silent means shutting up the critical thinking part of your brain. This is the challenge: listen to the silence.

Sounds super spiritual and strange, but I'm telling you this habit will help you. Not only does it give you the ability to completely clear your head, but it frees you from the pressure of the noise. If you can take the time to truly shut up, you'll feel your shoulders relax a bit. Suddenly, stresses you didn't even realize you were thinking about will fade away. Now, I'm not saying shutting up is going to solve all your problems. But at least it will give you a much-needed break!

Shut Off

Getting quiet means shutting off the things that make noise. This may seem ridiculously obvious, but it's worth reiterating. You can't experience silence and solitude in front of a computer screen. Just because you don't talk while watching Netflix doesn't mean you're actually practicing silence. Watching a screen is simply another form of noise.

Here is my challenge to you: If you're going to take the time to try this, actually do it. Don't just spend five extra minutes checking email in the mornings. Don't set aside a time to be alone on your phone. Shut everything off.

My personal rule of thumb is that if it has a screen, it's a huge distraction from silence and solitude. Often, though, I'll read the Bible on a screen. When I do that, I make sure to turn off notifications so I won't be distracted. The whole goal of getting quiet is to reduce input. Now, most likely you'll never experience zero input. Even if you eliminate every distraction, there's still the chance you'll hear wings flapping, leaves rustling, or the air conditioner humming. Those sorts of things are out of your control. But what you can do is eliminate the beeps and buzzes from your devices.

Technology is a great thing. It has done wonders for our society and our culture—moving us forward in ways we never could have imagined. But it has virtually eliminated silence and solitude from our regular daily habits. Resist the alerts from your devices. I promise you'll be okay without them for a few minutes.

Shut Down

One of the best arguments I've heard for practicing the habits of silence and solitude at the end of the day is the ability they give you to shut down. We've all had those days when work felt particularly long and draining. Then we had to prepare dinner, clean up after the kids, help them take baths, put them to bed, and suddenly we were completely wiped out. Those are the days when all we want to do is shut down.

I don't mean shut down in a negative sense. I'm not referring to withdrawing or avoiding conversation when you're hurting or upset. The type of shutting down I'm talking about is simply a way of unwinding from the day. It's putting the noise behind you and letting yourself lean into silence.

This may sound like something you can only practice at the end of the day, but again, it's up to you. Shutting everything down for a few minutes before starting your day may be just the practice you need. I'm not going to tell you when you should do this. Your place, your time, and your practice are up to you. I'm emphasizing the idea of shutting down so you know

Great leaders turn down the noise low enough and long enough to be ruthlessly curious about their emotions.

that silence and solitude don't serve as another place you need to get something done.

There's no pressure to perform within this practice. It's slow, it's silent, it's easy, it's relaxing, and it's rejuvenating. Maybe you need to give yourself permission to believe that. The noise of the world is never going to tell you this truth. Noise is inherently opposed to silence. But shutting up, shutting off, and shutting down are going to work wonders for your mental, physical, and emotional health. If you don't believe me, try it and decide for yourself. But remember, great leaders turn down the noise low enough and long enough to be ruthlessly curious about their emotions.

TRAINING NOT TRYING

Are you skeptical of all this? Does the idea of silence and solitude seem a little weird to you? That's okay. That means you're like me. At first, I wasn't convinced that all this was worth my time. Sure, I had heard successful people talk about meditation or yoga or whatever strange practices they did to get alone and get quiet. But I didn't buy it—until I tried it. And that's all I'm asking you to do.

This chapter is chock-full of practices and techniques that will help you experience the benefits of silence and solitude. But it's up to you to try any of it. I know a lot of people read books like this and think, *Yeah, that seems like a good idea.* And then they do nothing about it. The practice of silence and solitude isn't just a "good idea." It's a game-changer.

In John Ortberg's book *The Life You've Always Wanted*, he gives what is perhaps the most helpful advice for change that

I've ever encountered. He attributes it to Dallas Willard's book *The Spirit of the Disciplines*. I've read both books, and Ortberg summarizes the advice so clearly: "There's an immense difference between training to do something and trying to do something."[6]

If you convince yourself that great leaders are born through habits of silence and solitude and you jump right in, trying to become a great leader, you're going to fail. Why? Because these habits are hard. Really hard. But if you think of yourself in training, you're much more likely to get where you want to be. When, not if, you fail to spend as much time in silence and solitude as you think you should, you don't have to give up. You just have to convince yourself that you're in training. You haven't failed. Meeting with obstacles is only part of the training. And not giving up is part of the training as well.

In a world that is bustling and full and loud and exhausting, silence and solitude are the ways you can swim upstream. They are the habits that break through the noise and allow us to live life with a clearer picture of what we're doing on earth. But they're useless if all you do is read about them. If you don't do anything with the material presented in this chapter, it will simply become more noise in your life. So before you agree or disagree with the usefulness of silence and solitude, try practicing them. Then you can decide whether these habits are worth the effort.

CHAPTER 9

HABIT FOUR:
PRESSING
PAUSE

So far we've talked about the habits of finding simplicity, speaking to yourself, and getting quiet. Chances are, none of those were foreign to you. While you may have never practiced them or understood how they might work tangibly in your life, the concepts themselves probably weren't unfamiliar. Now we're talking about *pressing pause*. One of the strongest examples of pressing pause is found in the concept of the Sabbath. And if you're not a Christian, or if you haven't been around the church much, this one may sound strange. Even if you are a Christian and have been around the church a lot, you still might not know exactly what this means. We're going to fix that.

If you've noticed a theme in the past few chapters, you've probably realized that all the habits we've covered will create tendencies in you that make you different. Live like no one else now, and you'll be like no one else later. As cliché as that sounds, it's actually true. Or as Via Pullman (played by Izabela Vidovic) said in *Wonder,* "You can't blend in when you were born to stand out."[1]

Finding your *why* fights our culture's glorification of materialism and busyness. Speaking to yourself trains you to listen so you can understand your own thoughts—a counterintuitive idea in a world that is always trying to tell you something new. And getting quiet flies in the face of a loud culture that constantly demands your attention.

All these practices will help you turn down the noise so you can pay close attention to what your emotions are telling you. And if these habits have appealed to you because of their counter-cultural nature, then practicing this next one will be right up your alley. There aren't too many voices out there telling you the importance and value of pressing pause. But one voice has been preaching it for thousands of years. That's where we'll start to understand this practice, and then you can begin to incorporate it into your weekly routine.

WHAT DOES *SABBATH* EVEN MEAN?

To understand the power of pressing pause, we have to understand why the habit of taking a Sabbath has stood the test of time. For thousands of years, cultures have instituted and instilled the value of taking breaks from work for the sake of rest and reflection. The word may carry strong religious overtones; however, the philosophy of the practice of the Sabbath is embedded not just in our Judeo-Christian culture but also in almost every culture around the world.

Sabbath is a churchy word. I get that. It sounds like something priests and bishops understand—something the layperson might not be able to fully comprehend. And if you look to the modern church, you'll find a lot of different understandings and interpretations of what the Sabbath is and what it looks like in our lives. But I want to show you how the Sabbath isn't only about Sunday and it isn't only a spiritual practice. It's a personal discipline for the sake of becoming a healthier person, which will make you a better leader.

Sabbath isn't only about Sunday and it isn't only a spiritual practice. It's a personal discipline for the sake of becoming a healthier person, which will make you a better leader.

To practice it, however, we need a brief history lesson on where the Sabbath came from and what it means. For this, we turn to the Bible.

The Sabbath has actually existed from the beginning of creation. After God made everything, he took a day of rest. This wasn't because God was tired or because he needed a break. He was doing just fine. But what his day of rest did was set a precedent for people to follow. Remembering the Sabbath is number four in the Ten Commandments. God instructed his people to rest on the seventh day, and here is what he gave as his reasoning: "For in six days the LORD made the heavens and the earth, the sea, and all that is in them, but he rested on the seventh day. Therefore the LORD blessed the Sabbath day and made it holy" (Exodus 20:11).

God pointed out that the Sabbath started at the beginning. He designed rest to be a part of our nature. He made us so that we would need a day off. And if you've been going nonstop, you probably already realize this. So many of us, however, live as if a day off is optional. The weekend has turned from a time of relaxation into a time to catch up on extra work from the week and get ahead on what's to come. Our exhausting efforts have become their own form of noise.

I'm not saying everyone is a workaholic. I'm also not saying you need to stop working. Employment is a great thing. It puts food on the table for spouses and children (and we all want to eat). But do you work to live, or do you live to work? For many of us, work has turned from a *means to an end* to the *actual end itself.* Work-life balance has turned into work-work balance.

But it's clear that from the beginning of time, God designed life to look different. He designed us to need rest. He thought rest was so important that he even showed us what it looks like by taking a day off.

This isn't where the story of the Sabbath ends. The Israelites— the people God ordered to rest—took this command literally. On the Sabbath (which started Friday at sundown and ended Saturday night), they did nothing. I'm talking *nothing.* At first, this seemed like the right thing to do. God told them to rest, so that's exactly what they did. But over time, God's commandment became twisted and people added their own rules. Eventually, the act of resting took a lot of work.

The Jewish teachers of the law set up dozens of regulations around what people could and could not do on the Sabbath.

> But it's clear that from the beginning of time, God designed life to look different.

As a result, they couldn't walk certain distances, couldn't cook food, couldn't tend to their animals . . . the list went on and on. As you can imagine, trying to rest on the Sabbath turned into a somewhat tiresome ordeal. Then Jesus came.

If you read the first four books of the New Testament, you'll notice two groups of people Jesus was constantly up against: the Pharisees and the Sadducees. In many of these gospel stories, we see Jesus butting heads with them. One of their main beefs with Jesus was that he and his disciples didn't observe the Sabbath "appropriately." Multiple times, Jesus performed miracles during the Sabbath, which to the keepers and teachers of the law was a terrible thing.

But Jesus was pointing out that the Sabbath wasn't about a specific day. It wasn't about making a bunch of rules and regulations around this one day. It was about finding rest—the rest we desperately need. When accused of breaking the Sabbath, Jesus replied, "The Sabbath was made for man, not man for the Sabbath" (Mark 2:27).

What does this mean? Jesus was pointing back to God's original design. He was saying that God knew humans were going to need rest, so he created the Sabbath as a place and space to fulfill that need. The Sabbath isn't about a specific day. It's about intentionally pressing pause in order to rest in what we know to be true of God—that he designed us, that he knows our needs, and that he knows exactly how to meet those needs. J. D. Greear, author and pastor, describes the Sabbath this way:

> The point is not that Sunday is the new Sabbath and it now becomes the day upon which all Christians every-where must worship. The point is that Christ is Himself the

Sabbath, and if we are resting and rejoicing in His resurrection, we have fulfilled this Commandment. Even though we are freed from the technicalities of Sabbath law, we are still God's people, and we are still made out of the same stuff that Israel was made out of. This means we should still take one day a week to observe a Sabbath rest. But for Christians, the Sabbath means we rest in and remember the gospel.[2]

At this point I have to acknowledge that if you're not a Christian, the Sabbath might not make a lot of sense. We're about to transition into practical advice and what the Sabbath can look like today, but it's impossible to talk about the Sabbath without emphasizing the deeply spiritual components that make up this practice. When you establish the habit of pressing pause, you are training yourself to put your trust outside yourself. In a literal sense, taking a day to observe the Sabbath means trusting that God will give you the time and energy you need to get everything else done that week. This is no small feat. You're saying, "I trust someone other than me to help me do what I need to do." And that person is God. The one who designed us to need rest also designed us to find rest in him.

If you're not a follower of Jesus, first you should consider following him. As my boss, pastor, and friend Andy Stanley says, "Anyone who predicts his own death and resurrection and pulls it off . . . we should take him seriously." I believe following Jesus makes life better and makes you better at life. But if you're not a follower of Jesus, that doesn't mean you have to put down this book. And don't just take it from me. So many sources point to a weekly habit of pressing pause as a way to restart and refresh.[3] As we transition away from the history of the Sabbath and into the practicality of it, I believe you'll find several good reasons practicing the Sabbath will help you turn down the noise in order to become a better leader.

But here's the secret of the Sabbath: rest can be found, not at the end of a to-do list, but in the midst of everything you do. True rest isn't waiting for you just beyond the next deadline— it's not something on the distant and ever-elusive horizon. Rest is right where you are. If you can acknowledge that there is something bigger than you, then resting in what you do is possible. Followers of God realize they are small and inconsequential in his grand scheme. And this knowledge frees them up to rest—and to work diligently and faithfully, of course— while believing God is still accomplishing his plan and his will.

The Sabbath is a recognition of the tension that we are called to work hard but to trust God with our work. People who understand the Sabbath don't take a lot of days off to do nothing. Instead, they work hard with discipline and diligence while acknowledging that God's work is more important, and God's work always gets done.

This concept is crucial for leaders who live in a world of distraction, because escaping the noise and the busyness won't always be possible. Sometimes the noise is all around you and you can't get away. It's in those moments that finding rest will help you become a better leader. If this idea sounds interesting to you, then let's start by looking at it through the lens of another spiritual practice: fasting.

A FAST TO SLOW DOWN

Another practice of pressing pause is found in fasting. This spiritual practice has always intimidated me. Part of the reason for that is my great fondness for food. Honestly, I haven't missed many meals in my life. To the contrary, I enjoy them with solid regularity. After reading Walter Isaacson's biography on Steve Jobs, I ruled myself out as an entrepreneurial leader mainly because of Jobs's bizarre eating habits. If that's what it takes to create a life-changing product, I'll never be able to do that. (Now, to be fair, there's a wide chasm between Steve Jobs and me for many other reasons, and you should never rule yourself out because of eating habits.)

The more I learn about the power of fasting, the more I realize it's not only about food. If the original intent of the Sabbath was to turn down the distractions and noise for the sake of trusting God more, then fasting is simply a form of the Sabbath. Fasting may or may not be about food. Fasting from anything—whether food, social media, shopping, or work—is a practical way to implement the principles of the Sabbath in many areas of life. Fasting can be a way to turn down the noise in order to spark emotional curiosity.

The more I learn about the power of fasting, the more I realize it's not only about food.

Another way the Sabbath takes form is in *sabbaticals*. The concept of a sabbatical is based on the biblical practice of the Sabbath. In Leviticus 25, the Jews were ordered to take a year-long break from working the fields every seven years. Why? In an agricultural society, when you're not working the fields, you're depending on your sustenance to come from somewhere or someone else. Surely Yahweh was trying to help his people learn to trust him by turning down the noise and distraction that work could become. (More on the longer form of sabbaticals coming later in this chapter.)

One of our commonalities with the Jewish people from thousands of years ago is our fixation on work as a form of noise. And even though I've only heard of pastors and professors taking sabbaticals, I think the idea needs to cross over into every type of occupation. For me, the weekend provides an opportunity for a one-day Sabbath and sometimes a two-day sabbatical. Turning down the noise of work does something profound in me and teaches me three things.

1. First, it tells me that I'm not that important. When I leave work alone for a few days, I'm reminded that life is going to move along with or without me. The lesson that life goes on without us has a huge positive impact on our emotional stability and health.

2. Second, I learn that work is not my life. When all I do is work, my whole life is work. When I take a break from work, I'm able to put work in its proper place. My work and my personal life are not at odds. They are actually interdependent. I depend on them both for my life to be as healthy as possible. When I step away from work, I realize where work should be placed in the order of importance in my life.

3. Finally, taking a break from work teaches me to think about work differently. It allows me to think about it from a higher and broader perspective, which in turn allows me to see things about my day-to-day work that I wouldn't otherwise see.

A fast or a sabbatical doesn't have to be a certain amount of time, nor does it need to be relegated to a certain area of life. You can fast or take a sabbatical from anything that is allowing too much noise in your life. And when you turn down the noise, you give yourself the gift of evaluation.

> When you turn down the noise, you give yourself the gift of evaluation.

I am all for an *evaluated* life. Unfortunately, most of us fail to turn down the noise low enough and long enough to actually evaluate what's inside us. That's where the Sabbath can help. I never would have learned any of this if not for the idea of finding the Sabbath in fasting. When I considered the areas of my life where I needed rest, I was able to experience the benefits of turning down the noise in those areas. Entrepreneur and angel investor Timothy Ferriss fasts specifically from social media; he describes social media and the benefits of fasting like this: "It's just a low-grade anxiety that follows [people] all day, so it's become their new normal. When they take away the social media, even for 24 hours . . . it is incredible what a psychological relief it is and how much recovery it allows people to have."[4]

Ferriss has engaged in a few other fast-like experiences. He has slept on the floor for a week, worn the same clothes for a week, and eaten only Ramen noodles for a week.[5] He uses the term "voluntary suffering" to describe these types of fasts, which I think is a perfect image of what the Sabbath can look like. You're choosing to give up something to develop other strengths. You're choosing to turn down the noise so you can hear someone else. You're choosing not to do something so that you can rest. The weird thing is that self-development, listening, and resting sound like forms of suffering to many of us. A day off may sound like torture to you, but I'm telling you, it will change the way you live.

You'll see things you don't need in your life. Excess will become obvious. Unhealthy habits will show themselves for what they are. And you'll finally get some clear headspace to evaluate the way you're leading and living.

Of course, social media is an obvious example of a source of noise in our lives, and you definitely should try a fast from social media. But it's not the only thing you need to fast from.

What are the areas of your life where you need a break?

What keeps you from finding rest?

Can you take time away from that thing?

If so, what do you think the benefits will be?

That's the challenge. Pick something to quit. Not because it's bad, but simply to learn what you wouldn't learn otherwise. No doubt you'll learn something about yourself, and you might be better for it!

What's even cooler about the Sabbath is that it's not simply a way to quit things. It's also a way to start something new—like a new, healthier life rhythm.

FINDING RHYTHM

Fun fact about the word *rhythm*: I've never spelled it right on my first try. Something about it has never looked quite right to me—not enough vowels. Still, I know rhythm is a major factor in leading well. Making space for the Sabbath can help you find your rhythm, which will help you become a better leader in three ways.

Rhythm as a Way to Remember

Think back to when we talked about finding your why. The Sabbath may be the way to do this. Sometimes there's too much noise to truly answer the question, "Why am I doing this?" But finding space away from all the distractions can give you the chance to find your why. After you've done that once, you can stop finding your why and start remembering your why. This shift is subtle, but it's huge.

If you could find a way to remember why you were doing what you were doing every week, think about how much more productive—not to mention enjoyable—your life would be. I had a friend who suffered from what she called the *Sunday scaries*. Maybe you can relate. The Sunday scaries are when you get to Sunday evening and start to realize that the weekend is over and you're about to go back to work. If you're not looking forward to your job, then you might get a feeling of dread in the pit of your stomach. That feeling is the Sunday scaries. And if you're unfamiliar with your why, you may find yourself experiencing that sensation week after week.

Instead, taking time Sunday evening to remember why you work will help you show up Monday with a clearer picture of your goals, not to mention a better attitude overall. But that's only one example. Within the rhythm of your life, what do you need to remember about your why? What do you need to get away from to remember your why? For my friend, she chose to stop watching Netflix on Sunday nights and instead turned to

Finding space
away from all
the distractions
can give you
the chance to
find your why.

meditation. She stepped away from a distraction and toward a place to remember. What could that look like for you?

Rhythm as a Reminder

The Sabbath can also be a way to remind yourself of why you do certain things. This may sound similar to remembering, but it's different in that it doesn't necessarily relate to your personal why. Instead, removing certain things from your rhythm, or adding new things, will remind you of their purpose in the first place. We already mentioned my wife's experiment of removing social media from her life for a month. When she did that, she was reminding herself of why it was there in the first place. In that example, the reminder wasn't so much that social media was a felt need serving an obvious purpose. Instead, it was that other things were worth focusing on.

Another example is the idea of giving up sweets. When you do something like that, you get the space to remind yourself why sweets are there in the first place. Stepping away from them gives you the freedom to say, "I have sweets in my life to remind me to slow down and enjoy the simple things." Or maybe taking a break from sweets will help you realize that they take up too much space in your diet. The Sabbath helps you remind yourself of why things are there, for better or for worse.

It's not that you cut off all these "bad" things. It's simply that you take a step back to evaluate them. Sweets and social media can be great things. Or they could be things you don't need in your life. Neither of those options is necessarily right or wrong, but sometimes we need space from something to remind ourselves of why it's there.

Rhythm in Order to Replenish

To replenish means to fill something up again. Think about it like a bucket in a well. If you got your drinking water from a well, you would need to replenish your bucket regularly. Maybe a full bucket of water could get you through a few days, or even a full week. But if you never took the time to replenish it, you'd find yourself thirsty quickly. On the other hand, if you replenished your bucket every Monday and Thursday, you'd be good to go.

That's an outdated example—most of us have faucets now—but the truth is that many of us are living life with empty buckets. We're trying to do everything we can at work, at home, and in our hobbies, and we simply don't have the time or energy to do everything well. The Sabbath is a way to make space to replenish ourselves. If we aren't doing this, we won't have anything to pour out. Or if we only fill ourselves up with noise, then what we pour out won't do anybody any good.

This is where the Sabbath can be super helpful. Literally, the Sabbath is a time of rest. But the key here is to incorporate it into your weekly, if not daily, rhythm. Otherwise, it's something you practice only once in a while—usually after burning out mentally or physically. I have a friend who leaves work an hour early every Wednesday. He makes up for that hour on other days throughout the week, but on Wednesdays he always leaves early. For him, it's just one hour. That's all he needs to replenish himself and come back the next day feeling fresher. For you, it may be thirty minutes every day, or an entire day once a week. I can't tell you what's best for your life; you'll need to try different rhythms to find out.

After you have your rhythm, you can find places within it

to create some space. And you can use that space to remind you that you can afford to rest.

FINDING SPACE

While *Sabbath* may be an unfamiliar word for many of us, I want to close with a slightly more recognizable idea: sabbatical. You may recognize that as a professor taking a few months away from school. I want to argue that a sabbatical is something all of us can engage in. In fact, sabbaticals are already on our calendars.

The weekend should be a weekly sabbatical. We have already designated forty-eight hours to be work-free zones. Why don't we use them? For many of us, weekends may be work-free, but we've chosen to fill them up with dozens of other activities. These activities aren't bad, but they don't give us the space to realize what stepping away from the office for a couple of days can help us see.

I'm not arguing that you should pull your kids out of T-ball or stop making trips to Home Depot on Saturdays. Instead, I'm challenging you to look at one day of the weekend, or maybe one weekend of the month, as a time when you can step back. Because when you can create space between you and your work, you'll learn something.

Sabbaticals are especially helpful for super-driven people. They remind us that work still happens with or without us. I hate to break it to you, but when it comes to your job, you're probably replaceable. I know. That may be a shock to the system. But take one day off next month and you'll find out it's true. Everyone else will still show up and the work will still get done. This frees you up to ask: What roles in life are uniquely for me? The Sabbath will help you turn down the noise to determine the answer to that question.

Someone else will have your job or role someday. Think about that. Everyone's current job will eventually be filled by someone else. And if the future looks anything like *The Jetsons*, robots will probably replace us anyway. I'm kidding—kind of—but the point still remains. When we step back from our work, we'll realize two things. One, that we are

The world is bigger than what we're working on.

replaceable and the work will go on without us. Two, that the world is bigger than what we're working on.

Many of us live in such small bubbles that we forget what is going on around the world. Think about this the next time you're in traffic. Every other person in every other car has as much going on in their life as you do in yours. That person you walk past on the street has an entire life history that is as deep, complex, confusing, and interesting as yours—if not more so!

Pressing pause helps us see this bigger picture. Because the truth is, between the speed of the world and the noise of the world, we're doing everything we can just to keep up. We're going from work meetings to conference calls to PTA meetings to soccer practices to dinners to bedtimes faster than we can comprehend. And like Ferris Bueller said, "Life moves pretty fast. If you don't stop and look around once in a while, you might miss it."[6]

Making space for pressing pause is how you stop and look around. And it's not as hard as you think. Of course, we're not all tenured professors who get three-month sabbaticals. But we do have the margin in our lives to create space for all that we've talked about—we just have to find it.

The reason I think the weekend should be a weekly sabbatical is because I believe that's where you'll most likely find the space you need. The key is finding the best time to slow down. I'm talking slow. Down. Slowww. Dowwwn.

This could look like waking up an hour before everyone else on Saturday morning. It could be setting aside part of Saturday afternoon. Maybe Saturday night can be when you and your spouse set aside an agenda-free hour where you catch up and talk about nothing. Slow Sunday mornings before church can be a great routine. Or you could exchange an hour or two of football watching on Sunday afternoon for a time of reflection and meditation. And maybe Sunday night is the space where you never have too much going on and you can prepare for the upcoming week.

I don't know. Again, this part is up to you. But I'm saying if you don't take the time to find space, years are going to pass by without you noticing. That thought is scary but true. Today is the least busy day you will ever have. Life always gets busier tomorrow. Think back to when you were in college. You probably thought you were super busy at the time. But now you see that twelve hours of class a week plus six hours of homework and studying (*at most*) only makes for eighteen total hours. What did you do with all your free time?

In the same way, you'll look back on today and think, *What did I do with all that time?*

That's why I'm telling you now: Use it. Create space and let yourself breathe. It's too easy to fill every waking hour with noise. We've all done it—many of us are still doing it, and we have no idea how we're getting through each day. Life isn't about getting through. It's about living.

If we don't slow down, step away from the things we don't need, find our rhythm, and create some space, we're going to miss it. Pressing pause, on the other hand, can show us there's something more. And seeing that there's something more is exactly what allows us to turn down the noise and seek some rest.

CHAPTER 10

MASTER
CONTROL

Leadership doesn't have to be a secret. Enough material has been written on it to last a lifetime of reading.

When I made the pitch for my first book, the nearly eighty-year-old publishing vice-president said, "The last thing this world needs is another leadership book."

My first thought was, *Okay. Well, this conversation seems to be off to a good start.*

He was right though. Sadly, there might be more leadership books than there are truly great leaders. Because of that, I never wanted this book to be about *what* leadership is. You already know that. I wanted this book to be about how to grow as a leader. And growing as a leader is not easy.

One of the reasons leadership growth is so difficult for you and me is because so much in our lives resists growth. Growth requires change. Change requires giving up something today for something better tomorrow. Most people don't like giving up that kind of control. Actually, growing as a leader has more to do with control than most realize.

Growth requires change.

I know you probably realize this, but just to remind you,

something or someone is going to control you. It's already happening, whether you're aware of it or not. To really dig beneath the surface of growth, we need to answer some questions having to do with control.

What are you going to allow to control you?

Who are you going to allow to control you?

If you're not aware and intentional, your emotions will control you. The positive emotions want to keep you coming back to those same things that produced them in the first place. Those things that release the dopamine and serotonin will eventually form patterns of behavior in you—for good or for bad. They'll keep you coming back for more, and over time, they will take control.

But there's something about the negative emotions that keeps us coming back to them as well. You subconsciously hold on to unhealthy emotions because in some odd way, they make you feel better. The ocean of negative emotions wants to keep you angry or bitter or full of resentment, which will eventually show up in your actions and behaviors.

Unless you learn how to deal with how you feel, those negative emotions will own you like the substance owns an addict. You might be justified in hanging on to the emotion, but that doesn't mean it's healthy for you.

EMOTIONAL SOBRIETY

Negative emotions can be intoxicating. Whether it's the rage of anger, the bitterness of a grudge, or the self-loathing of insecurity, negative emotions work to create patterns of addiction inside you. And as with an addictive substance, the more you take the bait on them, the more your tolerance of them grows. And the more your tolerance grows, the more you create the patterns that keep you coming back for more.

Recently, I read a study that paralleled the three-stage cycle of drug addiction with emotional addiction.[1] It works like this:

1. Binge/intoxication
2. Withdrawal/negative affect
3. Preoccupation/anticipation

Dr. George Koob argues that taking the bait on negative emotions is similar to going on a drug binge. Then you experience a period of withdrawal and negative affect, the experience of negative emotions. Finally, after that wears off, the preoccupation with achieving the same high creates anticipation for the next time the feeling will return.

If it seems like I'm trying to scare you into paying even more attention, you're right. Look, this is the final chapter of the book. I sense the urgency of time running out with every turn of the page. This is my Tom Brady "TB12 with the ball on the last drive" moment.

To raise the stakes even higher, let me take another angle. Check out this powerful verse from the New Testament: "Be alert and of sober mind. Your enemy the devil prowls around like a roaring lion looking for someone to devour" (1 Peter 5:8).

The apostle Peter, one of Jesus's closest associates, didn't have the formal psychological training to identify the parallels of addiction and negative emotions, but he pointed out the threat in a different way. He compared the potential peril of negative emotions with the way the evil one prowls around ready to attack. No matter what you believe about God versus Satan, we can agree on a binary narrative of the world, which can be summarized as light versus darkness, good versus evil, or even Skywalker versus Vader.

Peter wrote that because this evil one is always lurking, we must both (1) stay alert and (2) keep a sober mind. Staying alert is key to not getting caught up in the euphoria of our own negative emotions. And keeping a sober mind—staying sober emotionally—will prevent us from becoming addicted to the forms of negativity that so easily entangle us. Emotional sobriety will enable you both to recognize the lurking lion and to avoid being devoured by said lion.

Being alert is about awareness, but it is also about self-control. The idea of self-control is that you actively and intentionally choose what controls you. You can willfully decide to be controlled by who you want to be, how you want to grow, and what habits you want to determine your future. By exerting self-control, you can refuse to allow the negative emotions that want to control you and have their way in you.

> Being alert is about awareness, but it is also about self-control.

Instead of giving in to these negative emotions, you need to handle them with a collar, a leash, and a shockingly strong invisible fence. They're addictive, they're dangerous, and they are not to be trifled with. And until you learn to turn down the noise low enough and long enough to be ruthlessly curious about your emotions, you'll never have the self-control to manage them.

UNDER THE INFLUENCE

As strong as negative emotions are, they were never meant to control you. And you are not meant to be controlled by them. Yes, your emotions are messengers, and yes, they are supposed to alert you of something—but they are not meant to whip you around. You are meant to live under a different control. The greatest problem with the controlling nature of negative emotions is that they keep you from being controlled in the way you were designed.

To think you are going to be free from control is a pipe dream. My worldview tells me that everyone is controlled by something. No one is completely self-directed. You have to decide what you want to control you and to what degree that entity will control you. Just as Apple's iOS, a mobile operating system, controls the body of an iPhone, something or someone will also control you. And this has everything to do with how you will grow and develop as a leader.

Here's another way to think about it: "Do not get drunk on wine, which leads to debauchery. Instead, be filled with the Spirit" (Ephesians 5:18).

This simple statement packs a punch, but don't be fooled into thinking that it is primarily about the use or abuse of alcohol. It's about far more than that.

As a side note, though, if you haven't spent much time around Christians, the topic of alcohol use is kind of hilarious. Living in the South and working as a pastor, I've become quite aware that nothing makes Christian people more uncomfortable than running into one another at the local package store. More specifically, when people from our church run into me at the spirit store (yes, pun intended), I always want to laugh at how awkward the interaction tends to be.

No, the reference the apostle Paul is making to alcohol here is really all about control. The first statement he makes about being drunk on wine is his way of cautioning those in the church at Ephesus to be aware of anything that seeks control. Sadly, the Pinot or the Chard is only one of the forces seeking to have control over you. Far subtler than alcohol are the negative emotions that will keep you coming back for more. Not only do they seek control, but they have the potential to whip you around for a lifetime.

Instead, Paul advocates for being controlled by someone who has your best interests in mind. He says you are at your best when the Spirit of God controls you. The greatest danger of being controlled by negative emotions is that you're missing out on allowing God—who incidentally created all emotions—to have control. The problem is not just the dangerous consequences of negative emotions, but the opportunity cost at stake when you miss out on being controlled by someone far greater. I know this may sound too far-fetched, too difficult to even comprehend, or maybe too religious for you, but hear me out.

At the very least, can we agree that something, whether your emotions or maybe even your own self-discipline, is going to have control over you? If so, then the next question must be: What or who is best to have control over you?

In my own leadership, there isn't always a clear intersection between my faith and the way I choose to lead. This topic of control, however, is one of those instances where my faith loudly and clearly informs my actions. When it comes to what or who controls me, so much is at stake. I could let negative emotions take control and experience loads of adverse effects. When I give free rein to my anger and cut someone off in a meeting, or when I give in to insecurity and passively work against coworkers, or when I let fear win by succumbing to self-promotion, I allow those emotions to control me. But it's worse than that. I miss out on something far greater.

Think about it for a moment: If Paul is right (and he gave his life for this) that the power of the Almighty is actually available to lead you and control you, why would you not want to tap into his leadership and control? Circumstances arise every day for which I need someone greater than myself to lead me. I'm too aware of my own limitations and shortcomings to not be open to giving up control.

Just last week, I had one of the most difficult conversations of my short career. I had to confront an employee about some behaviors that were affecting her influence within our organization. Having this conversation was going to be awkward and painful, but I was convinced that allowing this behavior to continue was failing both to lead and to love her well. Her decisions were eventually going to quell her own future and adversely affect those under her leadership. I had to have the conversation.

Leadership is best learned through experience. When it comes to hard conversations, I feel like I've been to the school of hard knocks where the school colors are black and blue. Sadly, I've made too many mistakes by relying on myself, being rushed, or reacting out of my own negative emotions. This instance was one of those moments, unfortunately too few and far between, when I had the awareness to slow down, quiet the noise, listen to what was inside me, decide how I wanted to lead, and prayerfully plan for fostering healthier responses.

Before the meeting started, I was able to yield my heart, my words, and my intentions to the same Spirit whom Paul referred to in Ephesians 5:18. I'm convinced this allowed me to care for the employee with so much more kindness, compassion, and empathy. Even though I was frustrated with her, disappointed in her lack of integrity, and dissatisfied with the way she had led her team, those emotions didn't whip me around. Obviously, conversations like this rarely go as well as we would hope, but after yielding control to the one who created my emotions, I was in a far better place to address the problem clearly and effectively.

MORE THAN YOU'LL EVER KNOW

The reason I felt compelled to put all these ideas to paper is because of how much is at stake for you and for me. If you never turn down the noise of the distractions around you, you will miss what's most important for your own growth as a leader. I deeply believe that learning to listen to what's inside

If you never turn down the noise of the distractions around you, you will miss what's most important for your own growth as a leader.

you and dealing directly with it are key to the continual growth I know you desire. In keeping with my love of lists, I'm going to end with these four areas of your life that I don't want you to miss out on.

1. Being the Best You

When you open yourself up to the idea of letting God have control of your life, I believe you are on the pathway to developing into the best version of you. No one knows you better. No one loves you more. No one believes in your potential more. As well as you may think you know yourself, finding the best you without the help of the One who created you feels like a blind pursuit.

> The best you is not a destination. Being the best you actually happens along the journey.

Plus, the best you is not a destination. Being the best you actually happens along the journey. Your healthiest emotional quotient isn't a destination either. It's a condition we must abide in. Just as physical health is a journey to be on but not a place we arrive at, so is emotional health.

2. Having a Vision for Your Life

My career seems to take a big turn about every four years. I've never planned for that to happen, but things have worked out that way. Every time a new opportunity presents itself, I come face-to-face with the same question: *God, what do you want for my life?*

It's a question of surrender. It's my way of saying, "I want what you want more than I want what I want." Without an answer to that question, I feel pushed and pulled by opportunities that

You can lead others better when you feel like you know where you're going in your own life.

may or may not be best. But the only way to get an answer to that question is to give up control and get out of the noise.

Don't be fooled: your future is neither more certain nor less certain when you have a vision for your life. But having a clear vision for where you think you need to go is vital to your leadership. You can lead others better when you feel like you know where you're going in your own life.

For me, I've noticed this miserable cycle repeating itself over and over again: The busier my life gets, the louder the noise. The louder the noise, the cloudier my future feels. The less clarity I feel about my future, the more I'm tempted to take the bait on negative emotions. Wash, rinse, repeat.

The same is probably true for you as well. I dare you to try breaking the cycle. Giving up control and getting out of the noise can move you from cloudiness to clarity and help you find a clear vision for your future. Your future is too important to miss out on it.

3. Caring Well for Others

You can't care well for others until you're caring well for yourself. To quote Lauryn Hill from one of my favorite albums ever, *The Miseducation of Lauryn Hill*, "How you gonna win when you ain't right within?" Such a brilliant question, Lauryn.

You can't win in helping others until you have dealt directly with the emotions inside you. The people around you are demanding that you get it right within so you can help them best. I'm telling you . . . it's possible and it's worth

> You can't care well for others until you're caring well for yourself.

it. As counterintuitive as it seems, you have to give up control to be able to get there.

4. Hearing from God

Finally, you'll never be able to hear from God until you turn down the noise. Hearing from God works in tandem with giving up control. The more you give him control, the more you can hear from him. Also, the more you quiet the noise, the more you'll want to give up control to be able to deal with what's inside you.

I've found that most of the time, the noise will be turned down one way or another. God doesn't often force us to turn down the noise. But he also doesn't want to have to shout over the noise. If he has something to say, he tends to stay patient with us as we stay distracted by our own lives. Eventually, though, when he wants to speak, he will. And if he has to turn down the noise to get our attention, he will. He loves us too much to not. Why make him wait? Why make him turn down the noise for us? Giving up control sure seems worth it to be able to hear from him.

THE FINAL COUNTDOWN

Leadership has an endgame. And it doesn't have to do with you. Leadership is always best when it's for the sake of others and for the good of others. Be clear on that.

Rest assured, though, you're not alone in this struggle. My hope is to rally a generation of leaders, young and old, who are willing to join me in the pursuit of clearer, stronger, distraction-free leadership. I want this generation of leaders to put their own ambition on the back burner and put the sake of others and the good of others at the forefront. The only way we can do that is by handling our own emotional health with the care it deserves.

And know this: you have a God who goes before you and who fights alongside you. I love this challenge and promise he gave to his people when they were facing literally one of their largest enemies: "Be strong and courageous. Do not be afraid or terrified because of them, for the LORD your God goes with you; he will never leave you nor forsake you" (Deuteronomy 31:6).

I look forward to continually leading others better, but I know my efforts are futile unless I'm leading myself as well as possible. The same is true of you. As attractive and addictive as the noise is, it can be turned down. Actually, it must be turned down. And when you can begin to habitually decrease the distractions and noise in your life and leadership, the world will be better for it! Let's raise the volume of our influence by turning down the noise!

NOTES

Chapter 1: The Danger of the Distraction

1. "New CareerBuilder Survey Reveals How Much Smartphones Are Sapping Productivity at Work," CareerBuilder press release, June 9, 2016, https://www.careerbuilder.co.uk/share/aboutus/pressreleasesdetail.aspx?sd=6%2f9%2f2016&id=pr954&ed=12%2f31%2f2016.

2. Erika Christakis, "The Dangers of Distracted Parenting," *The Atlantic*, July/August 2018, https://www.theatlantic.com/magazine/archive/2018/07/the-dangers-of-distracted-parenting/561752/.

3. Sydney Lupkin, "Can Facebook Ruin Your Marriage?" ABC News, May 24, 2012, https://abcnews.go.com/Technology/facebook-relationship-status/story?id=16406245.

4. Sebastián Valenzuela, Daniel Halpern, and James E. Katz, "Social Network Sites, Marriage Well-Being and Divorce: Survey and State-Level Evidence from the United States, *Computers in Human Behavior* 36 (July 2014): 94–101; https://www.sciencedirect.com/science/article/pii/S0747563214001563. The study, by researchers from Pontificia Universidad Católica de Chile and Boston University, compared state-by-state divorce rates to per-capita Facebook accounts. In a separate analysis, they also used data from a 2011–2012 survey that asked individuals about marriage quality and social media use. Their study found a link between social media use and

decreased marriage quality in every model they analyzed. They said their research did not prove that social media might be to blame for troubled marriages, but suggested such a link may be proven in subsequent studies. See also Everett Rosenfeld, "Social Networking Linked to Divorce, Marital Unhappiness," CNBC, July 9, 2014, https://www.cnbc.com/2014/07/08/social-networking-linked-to-divorce-marital-unhappiness.html.

5. Clive Thompson, "You Know Who's Really Addicted to Their Phones? The Olds," *Science*, March 28, 2018, https://www.wired.com/story/gen-x-adhd-screen-addiction/.

6. Thompson, "You Know Who's Really Addicted to Their Phones?"

7. "Deloitte Survey: Smartphones Continue to Reign Supreme as Consumers' Preferred Device," Deloitte press release, November 13, 2018, https://www2.deloitte.com/us/en/pages/about-deloitte/articles/press-releases/deloitte-launches-2018-global-mobile-consumer-survey.html.

8. Sean L. McCarthy, "Review: Gary Gulman, 'It's About Time' (Netflix)," May 4, 2016, *The Comic's Comic*, http://thecomicscomic.com/2016/05/04/review-gary-gulman-its-about-time-netflix/.

9. Nick Bilton, "Steve Jobs Was a Low-Tech Parent," *New York Times*, September 10, 2014, https://www.nytimes.com/2014/09/11/fashion/steve-jobs-apple-was-a-low-tech-parent.html.

10. Nellie Bowles, "A Dark Consensus about Screens and Kids Begins to Emerge in Silicon Valley," *New York Times*, October 26, 2018, https://www.nytimes.com/2018/10/26/style/phones-children-silicon-valley.html.

11. *Three Amigos*, directed by John Landis, screenplay by Steve Martin, Randy Newman, and Lorne Michaels (HBO Films, 1986).

12. Larry Copeland, "Atlanta's Ability to Handle Winter Storms Questioned," *USA Today*, January 29, 2014, https://www.usatoday.com/story/news/nation/2014/01/29/atlanta-winter-storm-response/5029489/.

Chapter 2: White Noise

1. "Distraction," Oxford English Dictionary, https://en.oxforddictionaries.com/definition/distraction.

2. M. Admin, "True Silence Will Drive You Mad," KnowledgeNuts, June 2, 2014, https://knowledgenuts.com/2014/06/02/true-silence-will-drive-you-mad/.

3. Stephany Kim, "Professors Cancel Class, Responding to 'Shocking' Election Results," *Cornell Daily Sun*, November 10, 2016, https://cornellsun.com/2016/11/10/professors-cancel-class-responding-to-shocking-election-results/.

4. I've heard Andy Stanley say this at least a hundred times.

5. Dan Rockwell, "Frustrated with Others but Comfortable with Yourself," *Leadership Freak*, October 19, 2018, https://leadershipfreak.blog/2018/10/19/frustrated-with-others-but-comfortable-with-yourself/.

6. David Moye, "600 Surfing Santas Make a Big Splash in Cocoa Beach, Florida," *HuffPost*, December 24, 2018, https://www.huffingtonpost.com/entry/surfing-santas-cocoa-beach_us_5c2136e3e4b08aaf7a8b855a.

7. Kerry Lotzof, "Bye-Bye Dark Sky: Is Light Pollution Costing Us More Than Just the Nighttime?" Natural

History Museum, November 16, 2018, http://www.nhm .ac.uk/discover/light-pollution.html.

8. "Light Pollution," Wikipedia, https://en.wikipedia.org/ wiki/Light_pollution.

Chapter 3: The Three Villains of Leadership

1. Fiza Pirani, "Atlanta Traffic among Worst in the World, Study Finds," *Atlanta Journal-Constitution*, February 20, 2017, https://www.ajc.com/news/local/ atlanta-traffic-among-worst-the-world-study-finds/ C6JR110E1z9xZeGGmjJ2HM/.

2. Dominika Osmolska, "When Children Lie They Are Simply Reaching a Developmental Milestone," EmaxHealth, August 9, 2011, https://www.emaxhealth .com/6705/when-children-lie-they-are-simply-reaching -developmental-milestone.

3. "UMass Researcher Finds Most People Lie in Everyday Conversation," EurekAlert! press release, June 10, 2002, https://www.eurekalert.org/pub_releases/2002-06/uoma -urf061002.php.

4. Kathy Benjamin, "60% of People Can't Go 10 Minutes without Lying," Mental Floss, May 7, 2012, http:// mentalfloss.com/article/30609/60-people-cant-go-10 -minutes-without-lying.

Chapter 4: The Me of Leadership

1. *Anchorman: The Legend of Ron Burgundy*, directed by Adam McKay, screenplay by Will Ferrell and Adam McKay (Apatow Productions, 2004).

2. My editor asked me to define this term for the older folks.

From the Urban Dictionary: "put on blast: to be called out for something; to have some information about you put out in the open in an embarrassing manner" (by Espe, November 22, 2003). See http://www.urbandictionary.com/define.php?term=put+on+blast.

3. Jeff Bezos, "2016 Letter to Shareholders," *DayOne: The Amazon Blog*, April 17, 2017, https://blog.aboutamazon.com/company-news/2016-letter-to-shareholders.

4. "Brian Regan—Learning Spanish," *Brian Regan: The Epitome of Hyperbole*, September 6, 2008, http://www.cc.com/video-clips/r3qlq6/learning-spanish.

5. Brené Brown, "TED Talk: Listening to Shame" (March 2012), https://brenebrown.com/videos/ted-talk-listening-to-shame/.

Chapter 5: Noise-Canceling Habits

1. William Harris, "How Noise-Canceling Headphones Work," How Stuff Works, https://electronics.howstuffworks.com/gadgets/audio-music/noise-canceling-headphone3.htm.

2. *Seinfeld*, season 5, episode 22, "The Opposite," directed by Tom Cherones, written by Larry David, Jerry Seinfeld, and Andy Cowan, aired May 19, 1994, on NBC.

Chapter 6: Habit One: Finding Simplicity

1. Andrew Stanton, "The Clues to a Great Story," TED Talk, February 2012, https://www.ted.com/talks/andrew_stanton_the_clues_to_a_great_story?language=en#t-466395.

2. Andrew Trotman, "Facebook's Mark Zuckerberg: Why

I Wear the Same T-Shirt Every Day," *The Telegraph*,
November 7, 2014, https://www.telegraph.co.uk/technology/
facebook/11217273/Facebooks-Mark-Zuckerberg-Why-I
-wear-the-same-T-shirt-every-day.html.

3. Brett and Kate McKay, "The Eisenhower Decision
Matrix: How to Distinguish between Urgent and
Important Tasks and Make Real Progress in Your Life,"
The Art of Manliness, October 23, 2013, https://www
.artofmanliness.com/articles/eisenhower-decision-matrix/.

4. The moose and the monkeys illustration was originally
inspired by a Russian proverb about chasing two rabbits.
See Chris Winfield, "Need Help Focusing? Think about
Two Rabbits," *Inc.*, July 29, 2016, https://www.inc.com/
chris-winfield/need-help-focusing-think-about-two-rabbits
.html.

Chapter 7: Habit Two: Speaking to Yourself

1. Good Life Project Podcast. Daniel Goleman: The Truth
About Meditation (A scientific look). https://itunes.apple
.com/us/podcast/good-life-project/id647826736?mt=
2&i=1000392373624.

2. Ibid.

Chapter 8: Habit Three: Getting Quiet

1. "Face to Face: Parents, Children Share Four Minutes of
Emotional Silence," NBC News, December 19, 2016,
https://www.nbcnews.com/news/asian-america/face-face
-parents-children-share-four-minutes-emotional-silence
-n693196.

2. Thomas Merton, "The Silent Life" (New York: Farrar, Straus, and Giroux, 1957), 167.

3. Jennifer Welsh, "Morning People Are Actually Happier Than Night Owls," *Live Science,* June 11, 2012, https://www.livescience.com/20880-morning-people-happier.html.

4. Donald Whitney, *Spiritual Disciplines for the Christian Life* (Colorado Springs: NavPress, 2014), 225.

5. C. H. Spurgeon, "Silence, Solitude, Submission," June 13, 1886, http://www.biblebb.com/files/spurgeon/2468.htm.

6. John Ortberg, *The Life You've Always Wanted* (1997; Grand Rapids: Zondervan, 2002), 30.

Chapter 9: Habit Four: Pressing Pause

1. *Wonder,* directed by Stephen Chbosky (Lionsgate, 2017).

2. Ed Stetzer, "The Sabbath, Jesus, and Christians by J. D. Greear," *Christianity Today,* May 16, 2014, https://www.christianitytoday.com/edstetzer/2014/may/sabbath-jesus-and-christians.html.

3. This article articulates it quite well: Christine Thomasos, "DeVon Franklin Lists Health Benefits of Observing the Sabbath on 'Dr. Oz Show,'" *Christian Post,* January 13, 2017, https://www.christianpost.com/news/devon-franklin-lists-health-benefits-observing-the-sabbath-dr-oz-show.html.

4. "One Tech Investor on Why You Should Take a Break from Social Media," WBUR *Here & Now,* February 8, 2017, https://www.wbur.org/hereandnow/2017/02/08/tim-ferriss.

5. Tim Ferriss Podcast

6. *Ferris Bueller's Day Off,* directed by John Hughes (Paramount Pictures, 1986).

Chapter 10: Master Control

1. George F. Koob, "The Dark Side of Emotion: The Addiction Perspective," PubMed Central, April 15, 2016, https://www.ncbi.nlm.nih.gov/pmc/articles/PMC4380644/.

How to Lead in a World of Distraction Study Guide with DVD

Maximizing Your Influence by Turning Down the Noise

Clay Scroggins

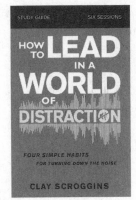

In this six-session video study, pastor Clay Scroggins builds on the principles he established in his bestselling *How to Lead When You're Not in Charge* and shows participants how to take the next step in their leadership growth by developing emotional awareness. As Clay notes, we are all surrounded by "white noise"—a soul-masking tool that keeps us from hearing the voices in our lives that we really need to hear. Our busy lives, the numbing nature of entertainment, and the urgency of ministry all work together to create a toxic cocktail of emotional distraction. And while many leaders have learned to tune out this "white noise," in the process they have become "deaf" to the inner issues to which they need to attend.

Emotional healing begins with emotional awareness—our ability to identify and understand our feelings. Developing such emotional awareness comes from engaging in spiritual practices such as fasting, meditation, Sabbath keeping, prayer, and hospitality. As Clay states, such practices today are often viewed as "countercultural," but they are solidly biblical and instrumental for helping us identify our emotions.

Through the practices described in this guide, leaders will unmask unpleasant emotions—robbing them of their stronghold—and learn how to pay close attention to the desires within. The result is that business, church, and ministry leaders will be empowered to replace the chaos in their increasingly busy lives with an emotional competence that leads to a calmer, less stressed, and more fulfilling life than ever before.

Available in stores and online!

How to Lead When You're Not in Charge

Leveraging Influence When You Lack Authority

Clay Scroggins

Are you letting your lack of authority paralyze you?

One of the greatest myths of leadership is that you must be in charge in order to lead. Great leaders don't buy it. Great leaders lead with or without the authority and learn to unleash their influence wherever they are.

With practical wisdom and humor, Clay Scroggins will help you nurture your vision and cultivate influence, even when you lack authority in your organization. And he will free you to become the great leader you want to be so you can make a difference right where you are. Even when you're not in charge.

Available in stores and online!

ZONDERVAN®
.com

How to Lead When You're Not in Charge Study Guide with DVD

Leveraging Influence When You Lack Authority

Clay Scroggins

One of the greatest myths of leadership is that you must be in charge in order to lead. Great leaders don't buy it. Great leaders lead with or without the authority and learn to unleash their influence wherever they are.

With practical wisdom and humor, author and pastor Clay Scroggins will help you nurture your vision and cultivate influence, even when you lack authority in your organization. And he will free you to become the great leader you want to be so you can make a difference right where you are. Even when you're not in charge.

In this six-session video study, Clay explains what is needed to be a great leader—even when you answer to someone else.

Sessions include:

1. The Oddity of Leadership
2. Lead Yourself
3. Choose Positivity
4. Think Critically
5. Reject Passivity
6. Challenging Up

This pack contains one study guide and one DVD.

Available in stores and online!